CW00816204

BIRKENHEAD

A HISTORY

Peter Burdett's Map of Wirral, 1777.

BIRKENHEAD

A HISTORY

ELIZABETH DAVEY

PHILLIMORE

2009

Published by
PHILLIMORE & CO. LTD
Chichester, West Sussex, England
www.phillimore.co.uk
www.thehistorypress.co.uk

ISBN 978-1-86077-491-1

Printed and bound in Great Britain

Contents

To my children, Francis, Katharine and Patrick.

List of Illustrations

Acknowledgements

In preparing this book I have received advice and information from numerous people. The staff of the following institutions have helped track down material relating to Birkenhead: Birmingham City Archives, Cheshire and Chester Archives and Local Studies, Dudley Archives and Local History Service, the Flintshire Record Office, the Grosvenor Museum, Chester, Liverpool Record Office, the Merseyside Maritime Museum, the Museum of the Isles, Skye, the RIBA Study Room at the Victoria and Albert Museum and the Watt Library, Greenock.

Among individuals I should like to thank Adrian Allen, Paul Booth, Dr Peter Gaunt, Dr Ann Kettle, W. Mark Lloyd, the late Dr Geoffrey Place and Alderman Arthur Smith, who all took the trouble to answer specific queries. The late Miss Marianne Laird gave me access to her collection of Laird family papers. The late Mrs Phyllis Hall allowed me to see the unpublished transcripts of the 1357 Forest Eyre, the work of the Ranulph Higden Society.

In both Birkenhead Reference Library and Wallasey Central Library, the librarians have been endlessly patient in providing me with information and seeking out illustrations. At the Wirral Museum, Hamilton Square, Ernie Ruffler has answered numerous queries on Cammell Laird's, whilst his colleagues have encouraged me with their cheery good humour.

At Wirral Archives, the members of staff have met my requests for material with infinite forbearance. In particular the former Wirral archivist, Emma Challoner, and her assistant, Francesca Anyon, were unstinting in their help. Without their support I think I should have got nowhere.

For the loan of photographs I was assisted by Birkenhead High School, Heather and John Chapman, Professor Peter Davies, Glynn Parry and Jenny Whalley.

For permission to reproduce maps, photographs or illustrations for which they hold the copyright, I must thank Paul Breen of the Boydell Galleries, the Friends of Birkenhead Park, Neston and Burton History Society, Longman Publishers, the Charles Thompson Mission, Tranmere Rovers Football Club, Wirral Archives and Wirral Libraries. In particular I am most grateful to Colin Simpson, Principal Museums Officer, Wirral Borough Council, both for his continuing encouragement and for permission to use material from the collections of the Williamson Art Gallery and Museum.

A special debt of gratitude is due to David Morris for his assistance with my illustrations and to his wife, Hilary for her generous hospitality.

Finally I must thank Heather Macfarlane, of Phillimore, for her skill and help with the layout and design of the book.

Thank you all very much. Any mistakes are mine!

Illustration Acknowledgements

Thanks are due to the following individuals or institutions for permission to use images for which they hold the copyright:

Paul Breen of the Boydell Galleries for the images on the dust cover and for figs 7, 41, 54 and 71; Neston and Burton History Society for fig. 34; Longman Publishers for fig. 4, from *Merseyside in Maps* by Patmore and Hodgkiss; The Charles Thompson Mission for figs 78, 113, 114; The Friends of Birkenhead Park for figs 155, 157 and 159; Tranmere Rovers Football Club for fig. 133; Wirral Archives for figs 29, 64, 79, 80, 99, 105, 107, 132 and 163; Wirral Libraries for figs 42, 76, 101-4, 137 and 151; The Williamson Art Gallery and Museum for figs 6, 33, 39, 44-6, 52, 56, 62, 68, 81-2, 92, 100, 119-22, 125, 135 and 146.

Introduction

Another glory on the Mersey's side:
A town springs up as from a magic wand.
Behold these noble docks—the merchants' pride,
And the fair park, extending o'er the strand.
The gallant bark that often had defied
The wild Atlantic, may no longer dread
The treacherous shore; in safety now 'twill ride
Within the waters of fair Birkenhead.

In the past the traveller to Birkenhead would have encountered very little. Surrounded by water on three sides, the blunt headland, covered in birches, boasted only a small group of monastic buildings, a scatter of cottages and a ferry house on the shore. There was no parish church, no great house and, even as late as the first census of 1801, only 17 families—a total population of just 110.

Over the next two centuries Birkenhead would expand from these small beginnings to become a major centre of shipbuilding, with thriving docks and substantial industries. It would boast the first public park, designed by Joseph Paxton, the first 'council flats' and the first tramcars to run in England. It would have fine buildings, its own pottery and tapestry works and an important art gallery.

From its schools would come such contrasting individuals as the poet Wilfred Owen, and the great Lord Chancellor F.E. Smith. Its Argyll Theatre would host performances by Harry Lauder, Charlie Chaplin and members of the Crazy Gang. From its shipyards would be launched vessels as varied as the early paddle steamer, the *Lady Lansdown*, the Confederate raider *Alabama*, the liner *Mauretania*, and many ships of the Royal Navy, including the two *Ark Royals*.

In both world wars, Birkenhead would share with Liverpool the agonies of a convoy port on the Western Approaches. In the 1940s it would experience the Blitz and in the post-war period it would, like so many industrial towns, face the well-intentioned havoc wreaked by the wrecker's ball. Shipbuilding, once the mainstay of the town, would face decline and the old

Borough would be absorbed into the newly created Metropolitan Borough of Wirral.

At the start of the 21st century, despite encountering so many changes Birkenhead still retains some of its past. The Benedictine Priory, its oldest range of buildings, is open to the public, while visitors can climb the nearby tower of the town's first church, St Mary's, to gain a view of the river. The Georgian elegance of Hamilton Square survives, as does the gridiron street pattern of the planned New Town.

Paxton's Park is newly refurbished. The Victorian Town Hall, no longer required for civic duties, houses the Wirral Museum. A section of the historic tramway has been re-laid and the Heritage Centre contains a fine collection of trams, buses and other vintage vehicles. On the Morpeth Dock a moving bascule bridge is in working order, as is the restored Victorian pumping station on Shore Road. With so much of its history still there to see, Birkenhead can look back over its past with pride.

1

Birkenhead before History

GEOLOGY

A modern visitor to Birkenhead, arriving by ferry from Liverpool, can stand on the Woodside waterfront and at low tide see shelves of rock jutting out into the Mersey. It is this rock, resistant to erosion, which formed the small promontory from which Birkenhead got its name—*bircen heafod*—'the headland growing with birch trees'.

To the same headland, in the 12th century, came Benedictine monks. The rock provided a 'dry point' for their priory and stone for its construction. In the bare floor of its ruins the bedrock is still visible—a coarse-grained, dull red sandstone, containing the rounded quartzite pebbles which give the deposit its name, the Chester Pebble Bed Formation, laid down in the Lower Triassic period 200 million years ago.

Similar strata form Holt Hill across Tranmere Pool to the south. Here the outcrop rises to some 50 metres. Bare rock is exposed in the gashes of old quarries, and road names like 'Quarry Bank' indicate where quarrying once took place.

To the west runs a sandstone ridge stretching from Bidston Hill to Storeton. Here the white and yellow rocks are part of the Helsby Sandstone Formation known by geologists as the Thurstaston Member. This ridge was also quarried. At Flaybrick a tramway carried stone down to Wallasey Pool. In 1848 workmen quarrying there found examples of the famous 'footprint beds'. Similar discoveries had been made earlier at Storeton. These beds preserved the raised footmarks of a giant reptile, *Chirotherium*.

Chirotherium was a creature similar to, but earlier than, the dinosaurs. Its name means 'Hand animal'. The rock containing its footmarks was laid down as sediment in arid and semi-arid conditions, similar to those of modern Egypt. The land surface, though desert, was crossed by rivers which occasionally flooded, forming temporary lakes. It was in the rippled mud of the lakeshore that *Chirotherium* left its footprints. So, too, did the smaller three-toed *Rhincosaurus*. As the mud dried, the footprints and ripple marks filled with windblown sand and this hardened to form sandstone which, when split, revealed casts of the tracks. Slabs of stone containing footprints are on display in the Wirral Museum and in Birkenhead Priory.

Sandstone underlies the rest of Birkenhead but is hidden beneath a mantle of glacial drift. During the Pleistocene

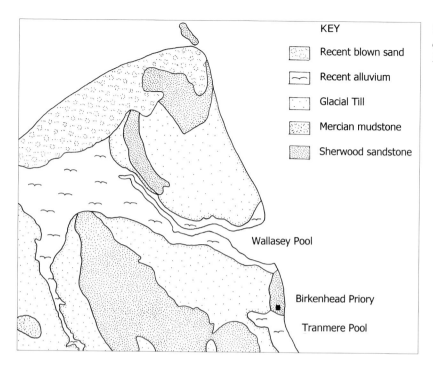

KEY

Recent blown sand

Recent alluvium

Glacial Till

Mercian mudstone

Sherwood sandstone

Wallasey Pool

Birkenhead Priory

Tranmere Pool

1 *Map showing exposed rock in the Birkenhead district.*

2 *Casts of the footprints of* Chirotherium.

3 *Sandstone visible in the old quarry face at the Arno.*

Geological Succession with revised Triassic terminology

Alluvium
Peat
Glacial Till

UNCONFORMITY

Mercia Mudstone Group	
Sherwood Sandstone Group	Helsby Sandstone Formation
	- Thuraston Member
	Chester Pebble Beds Formation

or Ice Age, ice sheets swept in from the Irish Sea Basin, coating the land surface with material brought from places as distant as the Lake District and southern Scotland. These deposits consist of coarse, pebbly clay, reddish brown in colour and plastic in texture. They cover most of the lower ground from the slopes of the Bidston ridge down to Wallasey Pool. As the town expanded, the clay was used extensively for brick making.

Above the clay are deposits of estuarine silt or alluvium, carried down by the streams flowing into Wallasey and Tranmere Pools. Interspersed with the alluvium are patches of peat, which in the past was dug for fuel.

THE SHAPE OF THE LAND

Today buildings cover much of the district, and the original shoreline has been almost obliterated by docks and shipyards. Fortunately a detailed survey was made before most of these changes took place. The surveyor was William Lawton, land agent to the lord of the manor, Francis Richard Price, and his plan was published in January 1824.

It shows Birkenhead, a small blunt headland, jutting out into the Mersey. To the north is the tidal inlet of Wallasey Pool, to the south the smaller creek of Birkenhead or Tranmere Pool. Originally both pools dried out at low tide, exposing extensive areas of sand and mudflats. Along the Woodside foreshore was a beach, with interspersed sand and rock. Upstream and not shown on the plan was Tranmere Sloyne, a safe deep water anchorage sheltered from the prevailing westerly wind.

It was possibly the sandbanks that gave Tranmere Pool its name. Though rare today, cranes formed part of the breeding waterbird population of pre-Norman England, and Tranmere may have indeed been the 'crane's sandbank'.

The area had few streams. To the south, a steep-sided watercourse, long since culverted, flowed along the line of Borough Road into the head of Tranmere Pool. Its sinuous course is still traceable on maps, since it formed the township and parish boundary. The Victorians called it Happy Valley and this name survives in the villa, Valley Lodge.

To the north, the Bridge End Brook, the Gill Brook and some unnamed streams flowed into Wallasey Pool. Reminders of these now vanished watercourses still reappear after periods of heavy rain. The line of the Gill Brook formed the parish and township

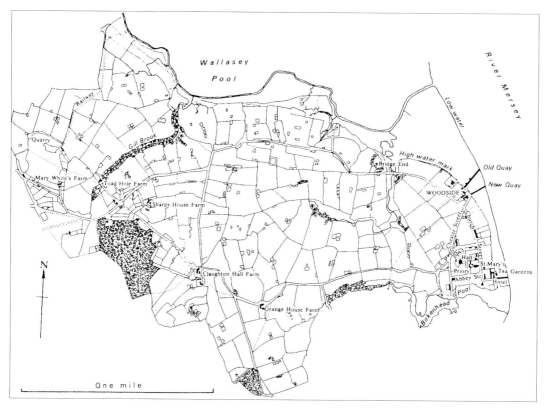

4   *William Lawton's map of Birkenhead, surveyed in 1823.*

boundary between Claughton and the ancient area of Birkenhead.

Much of the Borough is level and low-lying, reaching to just some 15 metres above sea level. To the west it slopes up to the more elevated ground of the sandstone ridge, reaching some 60 to 70 metres at Bidston Hill and the Arno.

NATURAL VEGETATION

Before the spread of roads and housing, Birkenhead embraced a variety of natural landscapes. The thin dry soils of the sandstone ridge supported lowland heath and pine; the hill slopes and the steep-sided valleys, like the Gillbrook, were wooded. The low-lying claylands were utilised mainly for grass, with marl pits a feature of many fields. The

waterlogged area of Bidston Moss, adjacent to Wallasey Pool, was an area of tidal flats and salt marsh.

Evidence of these varied habitats can be found in the field names on Lawton's survey: *Heath Hay*, *Big* and *Little Broom*, *Gorse Field*, *Moss Meadow*, *Seven Acres Marsh*, and *Seals*, 'the land with willow trees'.

PARKS AND OPEN SPACES

Today several large tracts of open landscape survive as public parks, saved from encroachment by being brought into municipal ownership. The first was the pioneering Birkenhead Park, created in the 1840s and preserving as an amenity an area of low-lying meadowland which might otherwise have been engulfed by housing. This

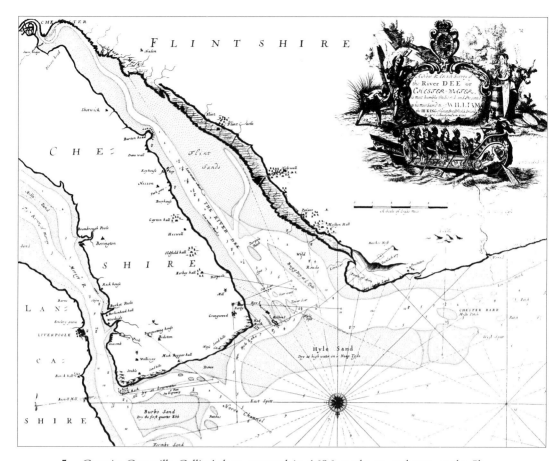

5 *Captain Greenville Collins' chart, surveyed in 1686, marks an anchorage at the Sloyne.*

6 *Early view of Birkenhead, c.1780, by Charles Eyes, looking across Tranmere Pool.*

7 *C.W. Clennell's view of the site of Birkenhead Park—low-lying land given over to meadow and pasture.*

8 *Mature trees in Flaybrick Memorial Gardens. The grave in the foreground belongs to the Laird family.*

was followed by Mersey Park, 21 acres, opened in 1885, Victoria Park, 29 acres, opened in 1901 and the Arno, six acres of former quarry in Oxton. Finally, as the boundaries of the Borough expanded, came the purchase of the 425 acres of Arrowe Park in 1927.

Birkenhead Park, especially, benefited from a major planting of trees and shrubs, many of them exotic species. Similar planting of specimen trees was undertaken in Flaybrick Cemetery, opened in 1864. Here, despite years of neglect and vandalism, sufficient ornamental varieties still line the paths between the grave plots to have gained for the cemetery, now renamed Flaybrick Memorial Gardens, the status of an arboretum.

Three areas of natural landscape also came under the town's control. In 1879 the Corporation took the unusual and far-sighted decision to oppose the enclosure of Thurstaston Common, an area of heathland seven miles to the

9 *Young trees colonising the former tip at Bidston Moss.*

west, but a popular destination for the Borough's walkers and picnickers:

> Having regard to the health, comfort and convenience of the inhabitants of the Borough of Birkenhead, and the benefits of the neighbourhood, about 60 or 70 acres of the highest and most attractive part of the common should remain unenclosed as a place of recreation.

The Land Commissioners were so impressed with the Corporation's case it awarded it 45 acres of the heath, 'to be administered jointly with the Church-wardens and Overseers of Thurstaston parish'. The award was confirmed in 1883.

A few years later, similar foresight led to the acquisition of Bidston Hill, part of the estate of Robert Charles de Grey Vyner. When plans for the Hill's development were announced, the reaction of local people was immediate. A committee was formed, chaired by the Mayor, and an appeal launched for funds:

> There is now an opportunity and probably <u>the last</u> that will ever be offered for the Public to secure <u>in perpetuity</u> the finest and most unique site in the district.

Contributions flowed in, the most generous being the £1,000 donated by W.H. Lever and his brother. In 1893 the council gave the campaign its support and in April 1894 the first 62 acres were conveyed to the Borough. Further land was added in subsequent years and the final eight acres in 1914.

A third stretch of unenclosed land lay along Wirral's north shore. Here, 54 acres of grass-covered dunes designated as the 'Meols Common Recreation Ground' were vested in the Borough following the Hoylake and West Kirby Improvement Act. All three areas remain open today.

Recently an unusual man-made habitat has been created on the unpromising landfill site of Bidston Moss, also once Vyner property. Originally very low-lying land at the head of Wallasy Pool, the Moss opened as a tip in 1936. For sixty years it received vast quantities of domestic and industrial waste, the mounds of rubbish finally forming a prominent hill. Since closing, it has been restored as an open space. Despite the problems of seeping landfill gasses and leachates, deliberate planting and chance colonisation mean the area now supports an increasingly wide range of plant species.

THE LANDSCAPE OF EARLY MAN

Ten thousand years ago the environment of the district was dramatically different from that of today. Sea levels were some 15-20m lower than at present, the inlets of Wallasey and Tranmere Pools were dry land, traversed by streams, and the Dee and Mersey estuaries were broad valleys rather than arms of the sea.

From about 8000 B.C. the climate became warmer. In response the vegetation changed. Open grassland was colonised by pine, birch and hazel woodland, then by a denser cover of oak, elm and alder. The sea level rose, periodically drowning parts of the coastal plain and causing conditions there to become increasingly waterlogged. Pollen grains from plants and trees drifted into these wetlands and were preserved in the layers of peat that were forming.

HUNTERS AND GATHERERS

Through this landscape moved small groups of hunter-gatherers, the Mesolithic or Middle Stone Age people. They had no permanent habitation but moved with the seasons to a series of camps, living off the local plant, fish and animal life. They used small stone tools or composite implements, such as spears, harpoons and arrowheads, made of tiny flakes or microliths of flint and chert, fixed in handles of antler, bone or wood. Flint was found in beach shingle or as isolated pebbles in the boulder clay. Chert came from Gronant, in North Wales, possibly acquired during seasonal migrations along the coast.

Stone is durable and scatters of microliths survive at several Wirral sites, providing evidence of a Mesolithic presence. At Greasby, only a few miles from Birkenhead, archaeologists have found evidence of human habitation dating from about 7000 B.C. Finds include burnt hazelnuts, numerous microliths, a hearth, stone-lined pits and areas used for food preparation and stone working. Similar sites probably existed round Birkenhead, but any trace of them has been destroyed by the spread of the built-up area.

Even without direct evidence, man's activity in the past can be deduced by analysing microscopic pollen grains preserved in local peat. Samples taken from Bidston Moss suggest woodland was being cleared from about 6000 B.C. The glades thus created would have attracted animals for hunting or alternatively provided grazing for domesticated herds. One way or another, the decline in tree pollen and the increase in pollen

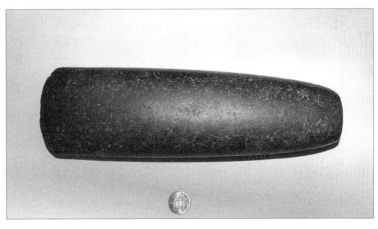

10 *This polished dolerite axe from Oxton dates from the period of the first farmers.*

from grass and weeds must have had a human cause.

FARMING

Evidence for a change in people's way of life comes from Bidston Moss, where the presence in the peat of a new pollen, *Triticum*, an early variety of cereal, as well as the pollen of arable weeds, points to the adoption of farming. The date of the samples lies between 4900–4500 B.C. The new economy demanded new tools to fell trees and work the soil. Archaeologists call the period of the first farmers the Neolithic or New Stone Age.

Chance finds in the locality provide examples of their tools. Stone axes have been found on the sandstone ridge and during work on the docks. The local stone is too soft for tool production, so axes were 'imported' from places with harder rock such as Cumbria and North Wales. The axe from Tranmere, for example, came from Great Langdale in the Lake District, and is of a type known to archaeologists as Group VI. Some axes, like the polished axe from Bidston, were so finely made they must have been for ceremonial rather than utilitarian use, symbols of status rather than tools.

METAL USERS

Metalworking began in the Bronze Age when bronze smiths developed the skill to produce high-quality tools and ornaments. The earliest bronze implements were flat axes which, like the earlier stone axes, were hafted on to wooden or antler handles. These evolved into palstaves, axes with a 'stop ridge' which made the hafting process easier. One such palstave was found during work in Birkenhead Park and

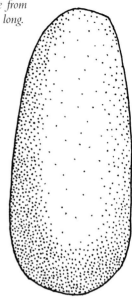

11 *A polished stone axe from Tranmere Pool, six inches long.*

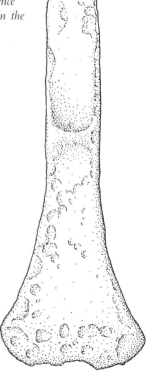

12 *A bronze palstave, found in the Park: evidence of Bronze-Age activity in the area.*

a short bronze rapier turned up in a consignment of sand from Storeton quarry. Stone continued to be used for tools and implements throughout this period and the shaft hole axe found at Tranmere dates from this time.

Finds from the Bronze Age are rare so we have to go to Irby, seven miles from Birkenhead, for more evidence of the period. Here a settlement was identified, with associated pottery, bronze-working debris and evidence of cereal cultivation. Radiocarbon dating puts the pottery somewhere between 1500 and 1100 B.C.

IRON

Further advances in metal technology came in the Iron Age (700 B.C. to *c*.A.D. 60), though finds of iron metal-work are rare. As with the earlier periods, one has to look beyond the confines of Birkenhead for evidence of what was happening at the time. Wirral lies close to North Wales, where hilltop enclosures abound. Nearer to home was the small promontory fort at Burton. It is not impossible that there were similar embanked enclosures on the Birkenhead side of the peninsula, but intensive development means that any trace of them is lost.

More detailed knowledge of the Iron Age has therefore to come from Irby. Here traces of late prehistoric domestic structures, oval or sub-rectangular buildings, have been found in association with other finds. These include a steatite spindle whorl, second-century B.C. in style, and fragments of so-called VCP, a type of very coarse pottery made in Cheshire and used to evaporate and transport salt.

One other site undoubtedly had links with Birkenhead. This was the beach port of Meols, which played a major role in trade from at least the late Iron Age. Undoubtedly some of the ships using Meols must have entered the Mersey, sailing to and from the mouth of the River Weaver, the main source of salt. Though it is pure conjecture, they may well have sheltered close to the headland of Birkenhead.

Despite the finds and sites discussed, the prehistoric population of the area remains largely invisible. All that can be said with certainty is that when the Romans arrived they found a well-developed agricultural economy based on stock grazing and cereal cultivation, and coastal settlements, including those of the Mersey shore, involved in seaborne trade.

2

Into History

The Romans

With the major legionary fortress of *Deva* (Chester) only 20km to the south, it seems likely that the Romans had some impact on Birkenhead. However, even before the fortress was established in the '70s, the Romans had a presence in Wirral. Finds from the Meols shore show there was Roman activity focussed on Liverpool Bay in the early invasion period, with evidence of trading even before this date.

Although Chester had its own quarries, the establishment of the fortress would have created a demand for high-quality stone, suitable for inscriptions. The outcrops at Storeton and along the Birkenhead ridge would seem to have provided this. Evidence that these may have been worked in the Roman period comes from a large sculptured stone of creamy Storeton-type rock, found rebuilt into the North Wall of Chester in 1887. The stone was the lower half of a monumental tomb. Its carved inscription reads:

> … Pub(lilia tribu) c(enturio) leg(ionum) V Macid-(onicae) et VIII Aug(ustae) et II Aug(ustae) et X V(aleriae) V(ictricis) uixit annis LXI Aristio lib(ertus) h(eres) f(aciendum) c(urauit)

Part of the original inscription has been lost, but translating the Latin abbreviations we find the stone dedicated to an unnamed individual '… of the Publian voting-tribe, centurion of the legions Fifth Macedonia, Eighth Augusta, Second Augusta, and Twentieth Valeria Victrix, lived 61 years. His freedman and heir Aristio had this set up.'

The centurion had served with the first two legions in Germany and with the Second Augusta at Caerleon in South Wales before being stationed at Chester with the Twentieth Legion. The style of the inscription suggests that the memorial was of early date. Other finds of cream-coloured stone, including fragments of a frieze and part of a mausoleum, may also have come from Storeton.

The Roman population of Chester would have needed more than stone and must certainly have drawn on the resources of its hinterland for food, fuel and forage. Despite this, the only hard evidence for the Roman period in Birkenhead comes from stray finds. In 1834 workmen quarrying at the Arno are said to have found a hoard of coins. The identification of these was unsatisfactory but included attributions to Marius (A.D. 268) and Victorinus (A.D. 268-70), suggesting a third- or fourth-century date.

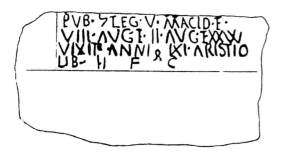

13 *Portion of a Roman inscription on Storeton-type stone, found in Chester.*

Perhaps the most significant archaeological discovery occurred in 1845, during the first phase of dock construction. The Chester-Birkenhead railway, opened in 1840, was being extended to Wallasey Pool, necessitating a bridge to take Bridge Street over the line. Foundations for this bridge were dug at just the point where the Bridge End Brook flowed into Bridge End Creek. As the workmen dug down into the silt they uncovered a series of oak beams, laid one upon another, at a depth of some 14 feet. A detailed drawing of the structure was made by the engineer in charge, a Mr Snow, and two papers reporting the find were read to the newly formed Chester Archaeological Society in 1850.

The author was the Rev. William Massie of St Mary on the Hill, one of the society's secretaries. He suggested the find was a Roman bridge, using the survival of mortise holes to support his argument. Though doubts were cast on this theory and suggestions made that the timbers might be those of a trackway or a waterside wharf, these have now been set aside and the bridge firmly identified as Roman. Routes from Chester to the north were vital to the Roman army. The main Mersey crossing lay well to the east of Wirral, at Wilderspool near Warrington, but the ferry route from Birkenhead may have had some local significance.

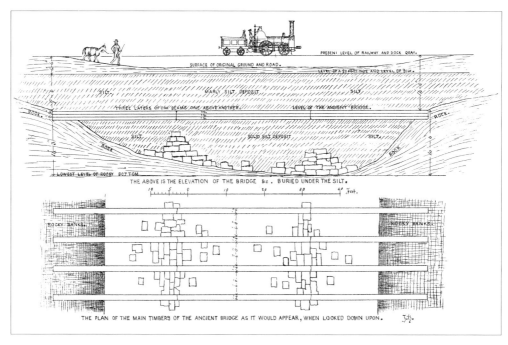

14 *Timbers from a Roman bridge were discovered in 1845, when the Chester-Birkenhead Railway was being extended to the Docks.*

Medieval documents refer to a highway in Birkenhead known as 'le Blakestrete', described as 'the King's highway … which leads from the county of Chester to Liverpool as far as Wallasey Pool'. Its name incorporates the element 'stræt', often evidence of a former Roman road. Part of its route can be traced, running in a straight line directly west of Bridge End and south of Wallasey Pool. Significantly, the present-day lane known as 'Roman Road', which runs from Storeton to Prenton, is not called 'street' and was probably only a medieval packhorse track.

That Birkenhead was part of a network of routes in the Roman period should come as no surprise. There is evidence of waterborne trade round north Wirral. One of the commodities traded at Meols, salt, would have passed the mouth of Wallasey Pool on its way from the Weaver valley. Similarly, ships bringing lead from North Wales must have passed Birkenhead on their way up the estuary. Finds of Welsh lead have been made at Wilderspool and in the Mersey itself at Runcorn.

In the rural areas, the pattern of settlement was probably one of individual farmsteads involved in a self-sufficient economy of pastoral and arable farming, continuing a way of life established in the Iron Age. As with earlier periods, one has to view Birkenhead in a wider context to understand what might have been happening at the time. To draw more than the broadest of conclusions from other sites and to relate these to Birkenhead is simply speculation.

THE SUB-ROMAN PERIOD

The centuries that followed the Roman occupation were once described as the 'Dark Ages' because of the lack of written and archaeological evidence from the period. Round Birkenhead it seems likely that initially there was little change as the local population continued as farmers, rearing stock, growing crops, speaking a Celtic language akin to modern Welsh, and probably practising Christianity.

Evidence for early Christianity in the area comes from the rare survival of a Celtic place-name, Landican, 'the church of St Tegan'. The name was originally used for the extensive parish of Wood-church and derived from its curvilinear churchyard, or 'Llan', and 'Tecan', an old Welsh personal name. Today the name Landican is confined to a small township and to the municipal cemetery that has grown up on its edge.

THE ANGLO-SAXONS

Landican apart, English or Anglo-Saxon place-names predominate in the area, despite its close proximity to Wales. Most common are the 'tuns', a place-name element meaning 'farm enclosure'. Examples are Oxton, 'farm or enclosure where oxen are kept', Prenton, 'Pren's farm' and the now lost Wooton, 'Wulfa's farm', a settlement once sited on the east side of Bidston Hill.

The Anglo-Saxons had come to Britain from the continent, settling first in the south and east of the country and subsequently establishing a series of kingdoms stretching to what are now the Scottish and Welsh borders. Struggles took place between the Saxons and British and between groups of the Saxons themselves, as different leaders sought to extend or retain their territory. One such engagement took place not far from Birkenhead in *c.*613, though recorded in the *Anglo-Saxon Chronicle* for the year 607.

Aethelfrith [king of Northumbria] led his levies to Chester and there slew a countless number of the Welsh.

This was the Battle of Chester, an encounter brought horrifically to life by the discovery of a mass grave on the banks of the Dee at Heronbridge. The battle cemetery, first identified in the 1930s, was rediscovered in 2004. It contained numbers of skeletons, all showing combat wounds, with many of the skulls cut clean through by the blow of a battle axe or heavy sword. The casualties were young males, all aged between 20 and 45. Carbon-14 testing dated their bones to the early seventh century.

Whether the corpses were those of vanquished Britons or Saxons was not established. However, with Athelfrith's victory the Birkenhead area came under Northumbrian control. This did not last long, and soon the Northumbrians were pushed back across the Mersey by the rival kingdom of Mercia, which spread northwards, including Wirral in its territory. Birkenhead, on the Mersey, the 'boundary river', lay at its frontier.

Initially the Mercians had been pagan, but by the mid-seventh century they had adopted Christianity. A commemorative stone set up by a local Christian community is in the Wirral Museum in Birkenhead. It is inscribed with runes and is one of the few pre-Viking stones from the North West. The inscription reads:

I F O L K Æ R Æ R D O N B E K
B I D D A T H F O T Æ T H E L M U

[…People reared this monument …Pray for Aethelmund]

The stone was probably brought from the site of the ancient church at Overchurch, demolished in 1813. Material from that church was used to build a new church in Upton, and the runic stone was discovered when this in turn was taken down. We know nothing of Aethulmund. He may have been the Mercian ealdorman (the highest rank of Saxon official) mentioned in the *Anglo-Saxon Chronicle* and slain in battle in A.D. 800. He was certainly someone of status.

THE NORSEMEN

A century on from Aethelmund's death, more incomers arrived. These were Irish Norsemen, who, as one story

15 *An Anglian commemorative stone with a runic inscription, originally from Overchurch.*

16   *Detail from the Overchurch stone.*

tells, were expelled from Dublin in A.D. 902 with their leader Ingimund. After an unsuccessful attempt to establish themselves in Anglesey they were granted land 'somewhere near Chester' by Aethelflaed, Lady of the Mercians. Other Scandinavians came from the Isle of Man and even from the Danelaw to the east. They settled near the coast where there were opportunities both for farming and for maritime trade. The extent of their influence can be seen in the distribution of Norse place-names, which cluster in north Wirral and along the banks of the Mersey.

How far the incomers created new settlements or simply renamed pre-existing ones is not clear. Certainly the basic pattern of townships seems to have been established by the 10th century, with Birkenhead close to, if not part of, a Scandinavian enclave stretching south to Raby, the 'boundary village' with its own 'Thing' at Thingwall, an assembly place equivalent to Tynwald in the Isle of Man.

The distinctively Norse character of the area can be found in the analysis of place-names. Though this should properly be left to the expert, it is possible to identify Scandinavian elements in names both in current use and on old maps and documents. Birkenhead, originally 'Birchenhead',

acquired a Norse pronunciation *bircen heafod*, 'the headland growing with birch trees'. Tranmere, first spelled 'Tranemol', was a combination of two Norse words, *tråna*, meaning 'crane', and *melr*, meaning 'sandbank'.

Even field names and those of minor topographical features show Scandinavian influence. One of the commonest is *brekka*, 'a slope', which can be found in Flaybrick and in the now lost *Knavenbrec* in Oxton. *Gil*, the old Norse word for a 'deep valley with a stream', is still present in the Gill Brook. The minor name *holm* or *home*, from the old Norse *holmr*, an island, is given to a dry site located in a wet area. Holm Lane in Oxton led down to the low-lying land of the Fender valley. Here also were Carr Bridge Croft, Carr Meadow and Carr Field Hey, all named from the old Norse *kjarr*, a marsh overgrown with brushwood. Similarly in Bidston there is Oxholme, the meadow for oxen, Bidston Carr and the Olurkar, the alder marsh.

This Scandinavian influence on local speech was to persist for years. Lanes were known as 'rakes' and as late as the 14th century fields enclosed from Bidston Moss were being given the name 'thwait', from the Norse term *þveit* meaning 'clearing'. Examples include the Great Thwaite, the Marled Thwaite and the Salt Thwaite.

17   *The miniature Viking-type hogback from Bidston, with end beasts carved in the form of bears.*

Though we know little of the organisation of the church in the pre-Conquest period, tangible legacies from the time survive in stonework associated with two local churches. From Woodchurch come fragments of a wheel-headed cross, and from Bidston a small carved hogback stone decorated with bears and interlace ornament. This hogback is similar to stones found at Brompton in the North Riding of Yorkshire and may commemorate a Viking who had trading links with York. Certainly it would seem to have been a memorial to an individual held in high regard by the local community, a member of the Scandinavian élite. A century and a half later a new élite would establish itself with the arrival of the Normans.

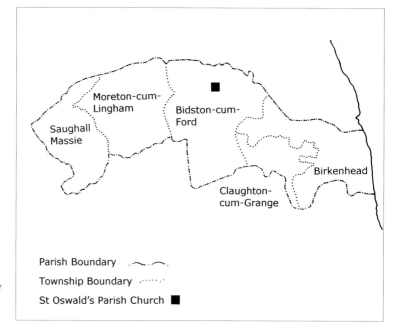

18   *Map showing the parish of Bidston and its townships.*

3

Medieval Birkenhead

THE DOMESDAY RECORD

In 1066, following the death of Edward the Confessor, there was a dispute over who should succeed him. On his death-bed Edward had nominated Harold Godwinson as his successor but Harold was killed at the Battle of Hastings and his place taken by the Norman, William the Conqueror.

At the end of the Saxon period Wirral lay within the bounds of Cheshire, a shire carved out of the old kingdom of Mercia and centred on Chester. It was subdivided into hundreds and the hundreds into manors. Domesday Book, written in 1086, provides a glimpse of life at the time. It records the names of manors, the Saxon lords who owned them in the reign of Edward the Confessor, and the Normans to whom they were given after the Conquest.

Birkenhead, as such, is not named in the survey. At the Conquest it is thought to have belonged to the powerful Edwin, Earl of Mercia, brother-in-law of Harold Godwinson. Most likely it was one of the unnamed manors which made up Edwin's large estate of Eastham, an estate which occupied most of Wirral's Mersey shore.

Following the Conquest, it looked initially as if Edwin might retain his estates, since he had reached an uneasy understanding with William. This was not to be. In the winter of 1069/70 William marched his army into the county, built a castle at Chester and established Norman rule. Edwin was killed by his own men and his lands, including the manor of Eastham, and therefore Birkenhead, became part of the extensive holdings of Hugh, the Norman Earl of Chester.

Hugh, in his turn, granted land to his under-tenants, including one Hamon de Massey, a descendent of whom later founded Birkenhead Priory. Domesday records that the first Hamon, whose principal estates lay at Dunham Massey, held seven hides in Eastham, a hide being that area of land which a team of oxen could plough in a year. This holding probably included Bidston, Claughton, Birkenhead, Moreton and Saughall Massie, all lands later acquired by the Priory.

Domesday provides documentary evidence of two other manors close to Birkenhead, Prenton and Noctorum.

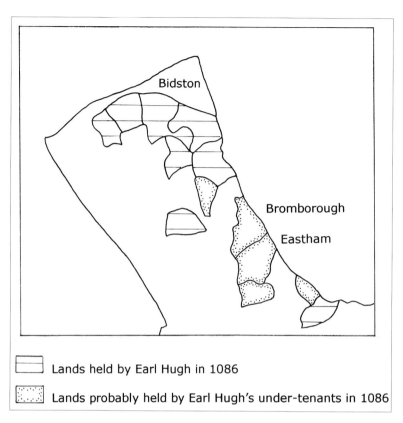

19 *Map showing Earl Hugh's manor of Eastham and the east shore of Wirral.*

Lands held by Earl Hugh in 1086

Lands probably held by Earl Hugh's under-tenants in 1086

Walter of Vernon holds PRENTON. Wulfgeat, Edric and Luvede held it as 3 manors; they were free. 1½ hides paying tax. Land for 3 ploughs. In lordship 1; 2 ploughmen; 2 smallholders. A mill which serves the court; woodland 1 league long and 1 wide. The value was 7s.; now 5s. William Malbank holds ... NOCTORUM. Richard holds from him. Colbert held it; he was a free man. ½ hide paying tax. Land for 1 plough, which is there in lordship, with 2 ploughmen; 2 villagers. The value was 15s.; now 10s.; it was waste.

From the stark details recorded by the Domesday Commissioners we can glimpse the basis of the economy: ploughs and plough teams, a mill, and some woodland. We can even deduce the disrupting impact of the Conquest in the figures given for the value of land. The general lawlessness of the area, the impact of an army in the field and the changes in land ownership inevitably caused 'waste'. As late as 1086, 20 years after the Conquest, there is still former farm land round Birkenhead not brought back into full cultivation. This is best expressed in tabular form.

Manor	Value in TRE	Value in 1070	Value in 1086
PRENTON	7s.	No value given	5s.
NOCTORUM	15s.	Waste	10s.
LANDICAN [Woodchurch]	50s.	Waste	40s.

20 *The Domesday entry for Eastham, with its reference to Hamon's holding of seven hides.*

Until the building of the Priory, Birkenhead had no place of worship. It formed part of the township of Claughton and, together with Bidston, Moreton and Saughall Massie, lay within the ecclesiastical parish of St Oswald, Bidston. The neighbouring townships of Oxton, Noctorum and Prenton and a small section of Claughton were in the parish of Woodchurch, and Tranmere formed part of the large parish of St Andrew, Bebington. Of the three, only Landican (Woodchurch) had mention of a priest in Domesday:

> LANDICAN. Aescwulf held it: he was a free man. 7 hides paying tax. Land for 8 ploughs. In lordship 1; a priest, 9 villagers, 7 smallholders and 4 Frenchmen with 5 ploughs between them.

> Value before 1066, 50s.; now 40s.; found waste.

THE PRIORY OF ST JAMES

The oldest doorway in Birkenhead is a small round-headed sandstone archway flanked by two windows. It leads into what was the Chapter House of the Benedictine Priory of Birkenhead and dates from the 12th century. Now surrounded by modern development,

the ruins of the Priory are the earliest buildings in Wirral.

Following the Conquest, many Norman barons used their new-found wealth to endow religious houses, first back in Normandy and later, as times became quieter, in their adopted country. No charters survive for Birkenhead but it would appear to have been founded

21 *Doorway to the Chapter House, the oldest part of the Priory.*

by a descendant of Hamon de Massey in the reign of Henry II (1154-89). Though Hugh d'Avranches, Earl of Chester, had re-founded the Benedictine abbey of St Werburgh's in 1093, there was no connection between the two religious houses.

The dates of the Masseys are obscure. We know that a Hamon de Massey granted the Priory the right to elect a prior from within its own community, a grant usually in the gift of the founder. Confirmation of this grant was given by Pope Alexander III (1159-81), which puts the date of the Priory's foundation after 1158. This would suggest that its benefactor was Hamon II, the grandson or great-grandson of the Hamon mentioned in Domesday. Hamon II died about 1185, a date consistent with the dates of the first recorded prior, a Robert, who was grantor of a charter dated c.1190.

As a monastic foundation, Birkenhead was not lavishly endowed. Its property consisted of lands spread through a number of Wirral townships including Claughton, the lost manor of Wooton, Moreton, Saughall Massie, Tranmere, Wallasey, Seacombe, Barnston, Higher Bebington and Bidston. Beyond the Wirral were lands in Lancashire and elsewhere in Cheshire.

Part of the estate was worked directly from its home farm or grange. This stood at the top of Grange Mount, on a site now bounded by Alfred Road and Euston Grove. At the Dissolution it was described as 'Birket Grange', and, later, variously as Grange House Farm or Grange Farm. It continued as a working holding until its fields disappeared under streets in the mid-19th century. Its name still persists in the township 'Claughton cum Grange' and in Grange Road, formerly known

as Grange Lane, the route that linked the Priory to its farm.

In the absence of any charters, the nature of the Priory's holdings must be inferred from an account compiled at the time of the Dissolution. Then the demesne consisted of

> one dovecote yielding 40s.; a water mill, 20s.; fish yards 6s. 8d.; two acres of meadow land 6s. 8d.; seventy-eight acres of arable land, £6 4s.; one parcel of land where flax used to grow, 3d.; the tenement held by Molyneux, 9s.; the profit of the ferry-house £4 6s. 8d.; and other small items, £14 14s. 3d.

Other land was leased out for rent, and these rents with the profits from the grange were the Priory's main sources of income.

Early in the 13th century an event occurred of enormous importance to the Priory's future. King John was seeking a safe haven in the north-west from which his ships could sail for Ireland. With Chester and the Dee controlled by the powerful Earl of Chester, John looked to the Mersey. Anxious to secure support on both its shores, he granted Birkenhead Priory a writ of protection in 1201, a privilege confirmed in the following year. Then, on 28 August 1207, he issued Letters Patent, establishing Liverpool as a borough with the right to hold a market. Attracted by the new town just across the river, the flow of travellers using the Birkenhead ferry greatly increased.

It was, however, demands for money from the cash-strapped Henry III which brought the Priory into direct contact with the Crown. Henry was embark-ing on a military campaign in Wales, and Birkenhead, like Cheshire's other religious houses, received a request for money and 'horses for drawing carts'. It was perhaps in recognition of this service that Edward, the King's son, granted the prior and monks Letters Patent and licence to 'assart' or clear their wood at Tollestow in the forest of Wirral.

Edward became King in 1272, and soon he, too, was involved in the conquest of Wales. In the late summer of 1275 he arrived in Cheshire. With few places able to accommodate the royal retinue, we find the King, in the first weeks of September, staying at the Priory and executing public business. Dates on documents prove his household was in residence on the 7th, 9th and 10th of the month.

Two years later Edward returned. Leaving Queen Eleanor at Shotwick, he arrived at the Priory on 31 July, staying for six days. One object of his visit was to meet envoys sent by Alexander, King of Scotland, to settle a boundary dispute between Alexander and the Bishop of Durham. On the same day, 1 August, 63 poor people came seeking alms and were fed at a cost of 1½d. each. How news that the king was at Birkenhead reached them or where they themselves came from is not recorded, but it must have been some feast! In the 13th century a man could live on 1d. a day; 1½d. was more than a daily wage. The total expenditure of 7s. 10½d. on the feast was recorded in the royal accounts.

The main purpose of Edward's journey north was to supervise his army in Wales. He had already initiated a major programme of castle building and he needed men, building materials, a means of transport and tools. On the other side of the Mersey, timber was felled in the forest of Toxteth and ferried to Flint on rafts. It seems likely that the rafts were floated to the shelter of the Wirral shore, before continuing round the north coast of the peninsula on their way to the Dee.

Edward's first campaign seemed successful but in March 1282 the Welsh rebelled. Immediately writs were issued demanding further services and supplies. The prior of Birkenhead, like the abbot at Chester, was called upon to provide transport. In 1284, swift to exploit this favour, he petitioned the Crown for permission to redirect a road that ran through the Priory grounds and to enclose the precinct with a ditch, hedge or wall.

The road in question was 'le Blakestrete', the main route to Woodside, described as leading 'from the county of Chester to Liverpool' and thought to be of Roman origin. Inevitably there were objections to the diversion, but the prior was able to cite his grant when accused of blocking up 'a highway which ran from Birkenhead, to the hindrance of passers-by and to the harm of the forest'.

22 *During the Welsh wars requests were made to the priory for 'horses for drawing carts'. This detail from the Bayeux Tapestry shows a horse pulling a harrow. The man following behind is 'broadcasting' seed.*

It was these same passers-by, many of them using the Mersey ferry, who in their turn were to cause hindrance to the Priory. By 1310 the burden of feeding and housing travellers was so great that the prior petitioned Edward II and his Council, explaining that as there were no lodging places nearer

23 *Edward I depicted in a stained-glass window in the former Birkenhead Town Hall. The window was installed after the fire of 1901.*

than Chester, 14 miles away, the Priory was often overwhelmed with 'sojourners'.

The famine years of 1315-16 increased the problem and in 1317 a royal licence was issued authorising the building of lodgings. A year later came permission to buy and sell food. Further favours followed in 1330, when Edward III granted the Priory the right to charge tolls to ferry men, horses and goods 'over the arm of the sea' to Liverpool. Monasteries were often founded with an obligation to perform some service to the community and there is a suggestion that the monks had previously been ferrying travellers across the Mersey without receiving a fee.

The rate of tolls was recorded at a Forest Eyre or Court in 1357, when the prior stood accused of excessive charging:

> for men on foot on market day ... a farthing, on other days of the week for a man on foot a halfpenny, and for a man on foot with a pack 1d, and for a man and a horse with a pack 2d and for a man with a horse without a pack 1d and for a quarter of any kind of corn a penny and no more.

On this occasion the jury upheld the rights of the prior to levy these tolls, and revenue from the ferry helped sustain the Priory until the Dissolution.

Over the years the numbers of travellers using the ferry increased as Liverpool rose in importance. The Priory itself acquired a burgage plot which gave it the right to sell produce in the town's market. This property was the site of its store house, described in a later document as

24 *A gold noble from the reign of Edward III, found at the priory. Though worn, the coin shows a boat similar to those that might have sailed on the Mersey in the 14th century.*

formerly the granary belonging to the prior of Berket in Wirral where such corn as they left unsold on the market days was carried up these back stairs of stone and there lay till next market day.

Despite the importance of the ferry, the Priory community never grew to any size. Records of the diocese of Lichfield show its numbers ranged between five and seven, making it the smallest monastic house in Cheshire. Also in the Lichfield Registers are lists of the priors, of whom 27 are known. Only one of these has a surviving memorial, Thomas Rayneford, elected prior in 1462. His stone grave slab was uncovered in 1818 by workmen preparing the site for the future St Mary's church. Its inscription reads:

Hic jacet Thomas Rayneford quondam bonus prior huis loci qui obit viii° Maii anno domini m^{mo} ccclxxiii° cuis anime propicetur Deus.

Translated this means: 'Here lieth Thomas Rayneford a former worthy prior of this house who died on the 8th of May in the year of our Lord 1473, may God be gracious to his soul.' The stone can still be seen reset in the Chapter House.

The minuscule nature of the Birkenhead community is reflected in its buildings, which followed the Benedictine plan. Ranged round a cloister only 60 feet square stood the church, the Chapter House, the refectory with its crypt or undercroft, and the western range which included the Guest Hall and Parlour. The church, unusually, lay on the south side. The kitchens, of which nothing survives, were separate from the main complex and a gatehouse lay somewhere to the west. Accommodation for everyday travellers was completely separate, possibly provided in the building that became the Hall. A detailed description of the whole Priory is given by Sir Harold Brakspear in R. Stewart Brown's *Birkenhead Priory and the Mersey Ferry* (1925).

THE FIELDS

Though the ferry brought in revenue, the community of the Priory and the peasants on its estates depended for their existence mainly on farming. Over the centuries land had been brought into cultivation and by the Conquest much of Wirral was under the plough. Some woodland survived. The very names Birkenhead and Woodside show that the headland was tree-covered until relatively late. Further evidence comes from field names like 'Wood', 'Further Wood' and 'Near and Further Holmes Wood'.

The farming economy was mixed, with its main emphasis on growing crops. Field names suggest that in Claughton and the neighbouring townships of

25 At the time of the Conquest much of Wirral was under the plough. This detail from the Bayeux tapestry shows land being ploughed.

Oxton and Tranmere the arable lands were worked co-operatively in large open fields or 'Townfields'. These were divided into unfenced strips or selions, known locally as 'loon', 'lawn' or 'loom'. Other names included 'Butts', small irregular strips, and 'Flatt' or 'Shoot, the word used for a block of strips.

In Claughton are 'Townfield' and 'Crooked Loons', 'Black Butts', 'Top, Further and Lower Flatt' and 'Long and Lower Long Shoot'. In Oxton

26 Tranmere Cross—Tranmere was one of the more populous townships of the locality in the Middle Ages.

similar names occur: 'Little Townfield', 'Crook Loon', 'Rabby Loon', 'Head Butts' and 'Flatt'. In Tranmere the Tithe Apportionment records 'Pike Looms', 'Wall Butts', 'Short Butts', 'Wood Butts', 'Greedy Butts' and 'Gall Butts' as well as numerous examples of 'Townfield', on the land later occupied by the Workhouse. At what point these open fields were laid out or when particular groups of strips were consolidated into single fields it is impossible to say.

Apart from the open fields one noteworthy enclosure was the moated site known as 'Moat Croft' which lay just south of Wallasey Pool. Covering some ¾ acre it survived until the 19th century, being marked on the 1824 Estate Map. Moated sites usually housed domestic or farm buildings and most date from 1250-1325. Like this one they were often located on wetter land.

THE FOREST

Early in the 12th century the whole hundred of Wirral was created a forest, one of four such forests in Cheshire. Ostensibly this was a punishment for the disorderly behaviour of its inhabitants and a way of providing hunting for the earls of Chester. The forest was not actually woodland but an area subject to forest law. Though primarily intended to preserve deer, an important element of forest law was the revenue raised through fining those who breached it.

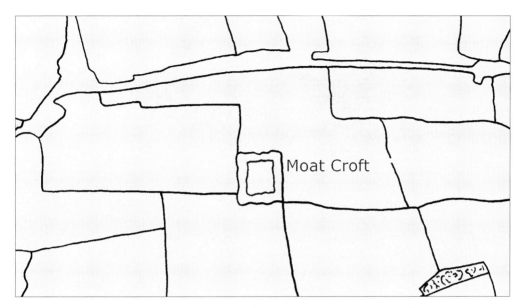

27   *Detail from Lawton's map, showing the medieval moated site, Moat Croft. The site is now covered in housing.*

The forest courts concerned them-selves with a range of misdemeanours, and many are recorded in the Forest Eyre Roll of 1357. One offence was the 'trespass of venison', or any activity which caused injury to the deer.

> In the 26th year of the reign of the present king … a doe was found dead in the fields of Claughton.

> A hind was found dead in a wide and deep turbary pit in the township of Bidston.

Another offence was the 'trespass of vert', the illegal damage or removal of trees and plants.

> John Starkey on the Tuesday after the feast of St. Mary Magdalen [took] a green oak in a place called le Lere in Tranmere wood in the Lord's enclosure.

> The prior of Birkenhead on Sunday before the feast of St.Barnabas the apostle … gave six oak saplings ['querculos'] to John Domville from his wood in Birkenhead.

More general were the offences known as 'purprestures', activities involving encroachment on the forest. The most common was 'assarting', clearing land to bring it into cultivation. Though the Black Death of 1348-9 probably killed a third to a half of the population, numbers recovered and the need to produce more food increased. Both prior and peasant appeared regularly in court, charged with clearing, enclosing and reclaiming land, and even draining the waterlogged stretches alongside Wallasey Pool.

> The same Prior 20 years ago assarted in the waste there an assart between the road which leads towards Chester and a wood, which is called Lassellesfeld, containing 6 acres, 1 rood, 10¼ perches which have 14 times yielded crops in winter and summer price 12d an acre.

The crops grown on such assarts are seldom mentioned. Some idea of what they might have been can be found in an order of Edward II, seeking 'wheat, barley malt, oats and bacons' for his army.

Other offences included cutting peat for fuel, digging for marl to improve the soil, and gathering gorse and fern:

> Thomas Prior of Birkenhead [and a couple of dozen others] were accustomed to dig turves in Bidstonwaste outside the covert that is Bidson Car … and to dig deep and large pits and to remove turves of their will to the harm of the beasts. Prior fined 12d and others 6d.

Building a piggery and keeping pigs was also a transgression:

> And the Prior of Birkenhead had 20 pigs in the woods of Birkenhead and Tranmere, price 5s … and the men of Tranmere had in the same place 12 pigs, price 3s.

Though the prior of Birkenhead was able to claim exemption from many of the forest laws, the burden of them fell heavily on the ordinary people. Equally onerous were the activities of officials, like the Stanleys of Storeton, appointed to enforce the law, who often abused their right to demand 'puture', food and shelter for their men and forage for their horses. It was a relief to everyone when, on 20 July 1376, Edward III issued a Charter of Disafforestation. From then on the people of Wirral were 'free to work and exploit their land' as they thought fit.

FISHERIES

An important source of food for those living near the Mersey was fish. There are records of boats and nets, but fish could also be caught in fishyards or weirs. Lines of stakes were driven into the shore and thin branches or withies woven between them. At high tide the fish swam over the stakes but as the tide retreated they were trapped and driven into wicker fish baskets. Legal disputes over 'lez fysshyardes' show that the prior, as lord of the manor, had the right to a proportion of the fish caught in this way, claiming all fish caught on Friday at the first or 'lord's' tide.

Oysters were also important and oyster shells have been found at the Priory. In 1759, long after the Priory had closed, Alice Price, the daughter of John Cleveland, let a section of the foreshore and bank of the Mersey near Woodside House for 'the intent and purpose of laying, keeping, breeding and propagating of Oysters' and making 'an Oyster bank or bed'. The rent for this was to be 'one good and handsome dish of ffish'.

28　*Extract from a lease of the foreshore for an oyster bed—The annual payment was to be 'One good and handsome dish of ffish'.*

4

Birkenhead
in the Early Modern Period

The Dissolution

In 1500 the lands of Birkenhead and its surrounding manors were still in monastic hands. In less than a lifetime all this would change. In July 1514, when John Sharpe, a monk at Birkenhead, was elected prior, England was a solidly Catholic country and the young King would soon write a devastating attack on Martin Luther, for which the Pope would award him the title 'Fidei Defensor', Defender of the Faith. There was no hint of things to come and Prior Sharp must have looked forward to a peaceful period of office, interrupted by nothing more eventful than a visit from his bishop.

Certainly, when Bishop Geoffrey Blythe or his representatives paid visits to the Priory in 1518, 1521 and 1524 there were no concerns. Blythe was Bishop of Lichfield and Coventry and the records of his visitations to Birkenhead confirm that the prior was well thought of, the rule of St Benedict was read daily and the silences were properly observed. The community, though only seven in number, was still recruiting novices and necessary repairs to the fabric of the monastic buildings were well in hand.

Evidence that renovation work was being carried out comes from a coroner's inquest. On 2 May 1524 a jury heard that Richard Hiccok of Claughton had fallen to his death from the scaffolding while working on the Priory. The inquest jury, made up of local men from Tranmere, Claughton, Oxton and Poulton in Wallaseye, found the cause of death to be 'mischance'.

Sharpe and his monks were not alone in thinking their priory part of the established order. In 1527 John Meols of Wallasey left the sum of 6s. 8d. to the prior for the painting of the rood-loft ('crucifixiorum') in the priory church. In 1531 George Booth of Dunham Massey left his best horse to the prior in return for prayers to be said in his memory. He also left ten shillings for a 'trentall of masses', thirty masses to be celebrated for his soul. No one could have foreseen that in a matter of years the Priory would be gone.

The first hint of change came with an Act of 1532 which ordered that money previously paid by English ecclesiastics to the Pope should now be paid to the Crown. Then followed a series of statutes that successively cut the ties between the English church and Rome. Prior Sharpe would now have to repudiate his oath of obedience to the Pope and acknowledge Henry VIII as Supreme

Head of the Church of England. More was to follow which would directly affect the Birkenhead community.

In 1534 Parliament granted the King a tax of one tenth of the income of all cathedrals, churches and monasteries. There had been no assessment of church wealth since the 'Taxatio' of Pope Nicholas IV in 1291 so up-to-date figures were lacking. Now commissioners were appointed, county by county, to inquire into the income of the monasteries, and in Cheshire there were 17, of whom three, Sir William Stanley, John Birkenhead and Ottwell Worsley, had the specific brief to visit Birkenhead. Here they questioned the Priory's lay steward, Randle Poole, on the financial state of the Priory.

One of the commissioners, Otwell, a 'clerk of the Exchequer', must have taken particular note of what he saw at Birkenhead, for it was his elder brother, Ralph, who was later to acquire the Priory's estates. The Worsleys were a Lancashire family and Ralph had an impressive title: 'Knight, Page of the Wardrobe and Chamberlain of his Majesty'. Clearly a loyal servant of Henry VIII, he was also 'Keeper of the lions, lionesses and leopards in the Tower of London, Porter of the Great Wardrobe, Controller in the County of Chester and Flint, Clerk of the Crown in Lancaster and Escheator in the County Palatine of Lancaster'. Ralph and Otwell died within two years of each other and both were buried in Chester at St Mary on the Hill.

By early 1536 the information from all the commissioners had been collated and edited and the *Valor Ecclesiasticus* presented to the King. Birkenhead Priory was not a wealthy foundation so its entry in the *Valor* is brief:

In the county of Chester, in rents and other profits anciently accruing as appears by the scrutiny and examination of the said Commissioners, to wit, Grange, or Ecclesiastical Lands called Birkett Grange together with the Water Mill and the Ferry Boat (*Molendino aquatico et le Feribot*)   £9   0 0
Lands in Moreton £3 4s 5½, Claughton £5 0s 4d   8   4 9½
Tranmere 17s, Haselwell 3s 4d, Brynstone 8d   1   1 0
Overbebynton 4d, Salghan 11s, Upton 3s   0 14 4
Davenham   0   4 0
                                                          £19   4 1½

There were also lands in Lancashire which yielded a rent of 15s. 2d. and a further £82 17s. 6½d. derived from the rectories at Bowden, Wallasey, Bidston and Backford. This gave a gross income of £102 16s. 10d., deducted from which was an allowance for the steward's and bailiffs' fees and certain other pensions. These figures show that Birkenhead was one of the poorest monastic houses in the county at the time.

In 1535, almost as soon as the first inquiry had been completed, Thomas Cromwell sent out other 'visitors'. They were to seek information on the running of the religious houses. Birkenhead, being in the diocese of Lichfield, was probably visited by the infamous northern commissioners, Doctors Richard Layton and Thomas Legh, who claimed to have visited 120 houses between 22 December 1535 and 28 February 1536. Whatever the truth of their claim, they appear to have found little to criticise at Birkenhead. Only one monk, Richard Chester, was described as 'incontinent' and there were no allegations against Prior Sharp. This lack of evidence, however, was not sufficient to save Birkenhead. The Priory, together with the other smaller religious houses with an annual income below £200, had all its estates confiscated.

Deprived of their buildings and lands, the little group of monks dispersed. The exact date of the Priory's closure is not recorded since no deed of surrender or inventory survives. However, in July 1536 Sharp was awarded a pension of £12, and in the following year he and four of his monks were sent to work as priests. With the community gone the priory buildings stood empty. The only people who passed by were travellers, one of whom, the antiquary John Leland, writing in his *Itinerary* compiled before 1543, noted that 'hard on Wyral shore is Byrket, a late priory of xvi monks … without any village by it'. He also reported on 'the fery house on Wyrale shoer'. He was wrong about the size of the Priory but correct that

the headland was more or less deserted. From the 'fery house' would develop the present Woodside.

NEW MASTERS

Following its suppression, the Priory passed into royal hands. Almost immediately its demesne lands were let to Ralph Worsley, who in March 1545 bought the priory estate outright, paying £568 11s. 6d. to the Crown. Worsley's new property comprised

> the house, with church, tower, graveyard, buildings, mills, barns, stables, dovecotes and garden within the precincts; a house tenanted by Robert Molyneux; a dovecote, a mill, fishyards, 2 acres of meadow, 78 acres of arable and a piece of land where flax used to grow, the ferry, ferryhouse and boat of Birkenhead, Bidston and Kirkby Walley.

29   *William Smith's map of 1598, shows 'ye ferry' at Woodside.*

He was also lord of the manors of Claughton and Woolton, where his tenants included Thomas Hiccocke, Richard Hiccocke, Margery Hare, Oliver Deene, Randle Drinkwater, Jacob Woodward, Roger Walkok (Willcock), Roger Watt, Roger Parbolt, David Woodward and Henry Deene. For these and the other former tenants the dissolution of the Priory and the expropriation of its lands meant little more than a change of master. Their rents, previously paid to the Priory's lay steward, now went to Worsley and, upon his death in 1573, to his eldest daughter Alice and her husband, Thomas Powell of Horseley, near Wrexham.

Other matters touched them more deeply. Despite Henry's formal break with Rome, many families had remained loyal to the Catholic faith. When, under Elizabeth I, orders were given to 'enquire into and punish recusants and priests', Catholics or 'recusants' were fined and sent to prison. From the local community, George Litherland, a weaver from Woodchurch, was accused of non-attendance at church and imprisoned, and John Hocknell of Prenton went to prison several times, finally dying in Chester castle from an injury inflicted by a keeper.

Though events like these were recorded, the daily pattern of most people's lives went unreported. However, probate records, wills and testaments and their accompanying inventories provide a picture of the way of life of the more fortunate members of the community. One such was John Penketh of 'Birkett aliis Birkenhead' who died in 1606. Much as a farmer today might invest in expensive farm machinery, so John's greatest asset was his team of oxen: 'ii oxen, whereof the landlord had th'one

for the hariott'. The 'hariott' or heriot was the best beast on an estate, which was paid as a kind of inheritance tax.

John had other stock, including horses, cattle, pigs and a flock of sheep. Some of the sheep went to his stepsons: 'Unto Richard and Thomas Charnock, my wyeffe's two sonnes, xii sheepes to be equallie devyded between them'. His own son, Thomas, was left £7, 'alsoe my table with frame and formes belonging to hit, and I give unto him more my greate brasse panne'.

John made one important bequest from which all his neighbours would benefit. Though the Reformation had brought an end to the celebration of saints' days, certain stages in the Church's calendar were still important and provided people with a holiday. One such was Rogation Tide, the fifth Sunday after Easter. This John remembered and in his will he left 20s. to his brother-in-law William Heare, of Claughton, so that '… uppon the Monday in the Rogation weeke, the sayd William shall p'vid drinke with hit for the Curatt of Bibston and the p'rishoners that com with hym, and that the drinke be drunken on the grene in Claughton, when the come thether as their accustome is …'

John was a prosperous farmer, styling himself 'yeoman' and with an estate of £151 19s. 10d. He seems also to have acted as the local moneylender, since over fifty people still owed him money at his death. Perhaps his bequest was intended to ease some old grudges. He could clearly afford to be generous. In contrast to John, a day labourer or even a husbandman would have had fewer possessions, and when sickness came, crops failed or there was no work to be had they had little to fall back on.

Trouble came in the first year of the reign of James I, in 1603. Plague swept through the county and local parish registers record deaths 'ex peste'. With farm labourers hit by the 'sickness', food became scarce and grain had to be bought in from neighbouring areas. In 1603 the price paid for wheat was 4s. 4d. the bushel, for rye and malt 2s. 8d., for beans 2s. 4d. and for barley and peas 2s. 0d. (a bushel being about eight gallons.) Twenty years later the death rate rose again following a further outbreak of plague and the poor harvest year of 1623-4. The crops had failed and food prices soared once more.

Some who died were buried at Bidston but others were buried in the little graveyard attached to the former Priory. The priory church had fallen out of use but the Chapter House, now converted to a chapel, still served the local community. By the reign of Charles I it had its own curate, Charles Adams. Born in 1598, Charles was the son of the rector of Woodchurch and later rector there himself. Educated at Trinity College, Dublin, his name appears as 'curate of Birkenhead' among the 15 clergy of the Deanery paying Ship Money in 1635. It was the levying of this unpopular tax that would within a few years precipitate the country into civil war.

'THESE SADD TIMES OF WARRE'

The control of lines of communication is vital in any war, so Birkenhead, standing at a key Mersey crossing, was caught up, if only briefly, in the conflict of the English Civil War.

For 11 years the King, Charles I, had attempted to rule without Parliament. To raise funds he had resorted to various dubious devices including levying Ship

30 *The exterior of the former Chapter House, used for worship after the Dissolution.*

Money. Demands for this tax, originally intended for a national emergency, were fairly successful in financial terms but were resented and at times the money became difficult to collect. Finally there was a tax-payers' revolt. Sir Thomas Powell of Birkenhead, lord of the manor and great-grandson of Ralph Worsley, reported that in his time as High Sheriff of Cheshire he was quite unable to raise money from anyone in the county.

The situation was the same elsewhere. In November 1639, when the sixth writ was issued, rich and poor alike resisted all attempts to make them pay. In the spring of the following year the King, increasingly penniless and with the threat of the Scots Covenantors, was forced to recall Parliament. Relations between Crown and Parliament continued to deteriorate. By the August of 1642 the royal standard had been raised at Nottingham and the country was at war.

31   *Sir William Brereton.*

Loyalties were divided, but there was little enthusiasm for a real fight. The city of Chester declared for the King, and in Wirral Catholic families like the Stanleys, Masseys, Hockenhulls, Pooles and Whitmores were also royalist. In general, however, Cheshire people were reluctant to engage in hostilities. So much so that just before Christmas a letter to the Irish Royalist commander, the Marquis of Ormonde, reported, 'Cheshire hath agreed upon a cessation of arms for a month'. [Letter from Arthur Trevor, 21 December 1642.]

In the New Year the tenuous truce was broken by the return to Cheshire of Sir William Brereton, the radical MP and a leading supporter of Parliament. Over the next few months Brereton waged a campaign in the county, rapidly gaining territory and establishing his HQ at Nantwich.

Surviving sources suggest no significant fighting reached Wirral, but Wirral men of the trained bands, a kind of territorial army, were mustered by the Royalist Sir Thomas Aston to defend Middlewich. Aston was no soldier and his men were both inexperienced and poorly armed. On 13 March 1643, after a battle of sorts, most of the force surrendered or simply made their way home.

Perhaps fortunately, the main action passed Wirral by, but across the water Liverpool fell to Parliament in May, and in south Lancashire only Lathom House, ably defended by the Countess of Derby, was holding out for the Crown.

The ferry crossing needed to be protected. By December of 1643 the prominent Lancashire Royalist and Catholic, Sir Thomas Tyldesley of Myerscough, was commanding a battery stationed close to the Priory. This 'kept a guard against Berket Wood over against Liverpool, having ordnance with them soe that they could and did shoot over the river to Liverpool towne'.

In the closing weeks of 1643 several thousand royalist troops were shipped from Ireland. In November some of their vessels entered the Mersey and it seemed that Liverpool might be attacked. The little garrison at Birket Wood waited expectantly but the ships sailed away, landing their troops at Mostyn in North Wales. On 25 January 1644 came news of their unsuccessful attack on Brereton's HQ at Nantwich. From now on Parliamentary ships would patrol the coast and prevent any further landings.

Relief for the Royalists came overland. In the summer of 1644 Prince Rupert, the King's nephew, retook Liverpool and soon much of Cheshire and south Lancashire had reverted to the Crown. Royalists in Wirral must have thought their fortunes had turned but events were soon to prove them wrong. In September Parliamentary troops crossed the Mersey and at Birkenhead captured the 'great piece of ordnance' which had been sent from Chester to cover the mouth of the Mersey. Arthur Trevor, writing again on 23 September, reported on the fate of the small force garrisoning Birkenhead Hall, the former priory guesthouse: 'This last night, the enemy possessed themselves of Berkett House, in Worrall, wherein we had a small garrison for the securing of the passage from hence to Liverpool, which will now be much more streightened than formerly and I am afraid will not last long.'

It was in fact a matter of weeks. 'Worrall is all lost to the enemy and plundered to the ground by sir William Brereton,' wrote Dr Williams, Archbishop of York, another correspondent of the Marquis of Ormonde, in a letter dated 30 October. By mid-November, after a 10-week siege, Liverpool surrendered to the Parliamentarian Sir John Meldrum. Parliament now controlled both sides of the Mersey.

In Cheshire, only Chester, less than 20 miles from Birkenhead, was still holding out for the Crown. On 24 September 1645 the Royalists, who had come to relieve the city, were defeated at the Battle of Rowton Moor and the siege continued. Finally, on 3 February 1646 after a terrible winter of hunger and hardship, the city fell.

The war and its aftermath brought disruption. With Parliament victorious, royalist estates like those of Sir Thomas Powell were confiscated or 'sequestered' and their owners had to pay a fine to get them back. In 1646 Powell paid £137 18s. 0d. for the Birket ferry and his lands in Claughton and Tranmere. The next year he died and his estates passed to his grandson, another Sir Thomas.

Everyone suffered as farms were plundered and families forced to provide free quarter for the troops. Evidence for this comes from a statement attached to a copy of the will of 'John Smith, late of Birkett-wood, waterman', dated 1648. In the statement his widow Maria explained how the original will had come to be lost:

> Aboute two or three months after the deceased's death [in 1648] … about two troupes of horse quartered att her house [at the Woodside Ferry] for aboute eight or nine days, in order to their transportation to Ireland, in these sadd times of warre, at which tyme being in great distraction, the said Will and Inventorie … was … lost and was never since found.

32 *Daniel King's view of the Priory, 1656, though lacking in accuracy, shows the damage inflicted during the Civil War.*

Another casualty was the Priory. Its buildings, round which fighting had raged, were in ruins. Daniel King's view of 1656 shows only the Chapter House and north range still roofed over. The rest of the buildings stand open to the skies.

Liverpool had also suffered in the Civil War, particularly in the sieges of 1644. With peace, however, its fortunes picked up and its trade with Ireland and across the Atlantic expanded rapidly. Birkenhead, on the opposite bank of the Mersey, though remaining small itself, inevitably felt the impact of the greatly increased volume of traffic on the river.

THE MANOR IN THE 17TH CENTURY

The first accurate survey of the waters round Birkenhead was completed in 1686 by Captain Greenville Collins, the Hydrographer Royal. Collins' chart shows deep water close to the head-land and an anchorage just upstream of 'Birket Pool' at the Sloyne. It also shows two landmarks, 'Berkenhead Hall' and Woodside, both marked by the conventional symbol for a house.

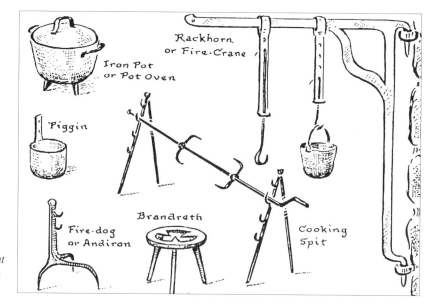

34   *Everyday items in use round the fire at the time of the Hearth Tax.*

The Hall, the possession of the Powells, was the successor of the old priory guesthouse. As 'Berkett Halle' it had appeared as one of 20 properties in a 1663 return of Claughton households, assessed for the payment of 'harth money' or Hearth Tax, an early attempt to relate taxation to the size of a householder's property. People with more than two chimneys were liable for payment and anyone who had blocked up a chimney paid double. The Hall, with only one hearth, was exempt.

Woodside was the departure point for the Liverpool ferry. The 'ferry, ferryhouse and boat of Birkenhead' had been acquired by Worsley, and he and his successors had been involved in numerous disputes over the rights to the ferry tolls. By Collins' time the conflicting claims seem to have been resolved and the ferry house at Woodside had become a sufficiently capacious establishment to accommodate the holding of the manorial court.

One of the few records of this court survives from the autumn of 1689, late in the Powell era:

> The presentment of the Jury of the Cort Leet and baron held for the Manor of Claughton cum Grange and Birkett wood kept at ye Woodside house the 22 of October for Samuel Powell Esq of ye Manor of Berkenhead.
> We present John Sirese for takeing in a inmake … 6s. 8d.
> Wee present John Sirese for a pound Breshe … 3s. 4d.
> Wee order ye Newefield Lane leading from Samueli Sharps to Thomas Charnockes to be repared betwixt [now] and Micellmus in paine of … 1s.
> Wee order the Ditch from ye pits of ye heath to ye corner of ye Lore Heath of ye side of ye lane next to

ye Gill Brucke to be done betwixt [now] and ye fife & twentieth of March in paine of … 3s. 4d.
> Wee order ye Ditch betwixt ye lane and ye Lore heath & betwixt Thomas Charnockes croft and Lore heath and betwixt Thomas Charnockes croft [and] Lasles Lea to be done betwixt [now] and May in pane of … 10s.
> Wee present Margaret Wilson of Walezy Junr for a pound Breash … 3s. 4d.
> Wee present John Wilson for incroshing of Clachon coming.
> Wee present John Wilson & John Leene Constables and Burleymen for Clachon.
> Wee present Thomas Charnocke, Burleman for ye demene of Berkett.
> Wee present ye Lord of the Manor & John Wilson for not repairing ye Malling hey Bridge, to be done betwixt [now] and Midsummer in paine of … 10s.
> Wee present Mr. Urmson for not repairing his bilding according to former order in paine of … 10s.
> Wee present William Webster for Breaking ye sise of Bred and Ale.
>
> [The original fines are written in Roman numerals.]

The running of this court was the responsibility of jurors, drawn from among Powell's tenants. The problems they faced were various. The lanes in Claughton required maintaining while neighbouring ditches and water courses had to be kept clear. The bridge at Bridge End needed repair. Animals had strayed onto the open fields and been impounded in the pinfold. Individuals had encroached on the common or allowed their building to fall into disrepair. John Sires had taken in a lodger or 'inmake', a stranger from elsewhere, who it was feared might become a burden on the

35   *The former Toad Hole Farm, Tollemache Road, one of the farms of the manor.*

Shortly after this, Samuel Powell seems to have fallen into financial difficulties. These were so serious that a private Act of Parliament, the Powell's Estate Act of 1695, was passed which placed Birkenhead and Claughton in the hands of trustees. Powell had no children but by his will, dated 16 March 1705, his estates were left to the families of his two nieces. It was they who negotiated the sale of the manor to the Liverpool merchant John Cleievland (or Cleveland) in 1707. Cleveland had been mayor of Liverpool in 1703 and became its MP in 1710. At his death in 1716 his estate passed first to his sons, both of whom died childless, and then in 1734 to his daughter Alice. It was Francis Richard Price, the great-grandson of Alice through her second husband, Francis Price of Bryn-y-Pys, near Overton in Flintshire, who a century later was to oversee great changes in Birkenhead.

township. William Webster had broken the assize of bread and ale, baking or brewing bread and ale without a license or producing goods of poor quality. These were all minor offences, typical of many farming communities. More serious crimes would be dealt with by the courts in Chester.

36   *An 18th-century engraving of the priory ruins.*

5

A Town is Born

From the turn of the 18th century, views across the Mersey, looking from Birkenhead, show a river thronging with ships of all sizes. Celia Fiennes, that intrepid lady traveller, had to cross this river on her great journey round the country in 1698. As she travelled the eight miles from Burton to the ferry on horseback, the landscape through which she passed was still rural, a scatter of farms and cottages housing a population mostly earning their living directly from the land.

In Birkenhead, although farming still predominated, proximity to the now burgeoning port of Liverpool added an extra dimension to the economy. Boatmen, mariners and others engaged in maritime trades appear in increasing numbers in the records. One such boatman would have transported Celia and her horses across the river. Her description of the crossing from Birkenhead is vivid:

> The mouth of the river by reason of the sands and rocks is a gate to the river; this I ferried over and was an hour and halfe in the passage, its of great bredth and at low water is so deep and salt as the sea almost, though it does not cast so green a hew on the water as the sea, but else the waves toss and the rocks great all round it and is as dangerous as the sea; its in a sort of Hoy that I ferried over and my horses, the boat would have held 100 people.

Another traveller was Daniel Defoe:

> Here is a ferry over the Mersey, which at full sea is more than two miles over. We land on the flat shore on the other side, and are contented to ride through the water for some length, not on horseback but on the shoulders of some Lancashire clown …

Other visitors left a visual record. Samuel Buck based his famous print 'The South West Prospect of Liverpoole …' of 1728 on the view from Birkenhead. He also drew the Priory. Though mainly in ruins, one building still stood roofed over and in reasonable order. This was the former Chapter House, now licensed as a chapel of ease to the church of St Oswald's, Bidston. From its records we get a glimpse of the small community who worshipped there. The main events of their lives—baptisms, marriages and funerals—are recorded in its registers.

The first burial was that of the 'Revd Robert Janny, clerk, Minister of Birkenhead and Overchurch', interred

37

37 *Vessels on the Mersey—Detail from the Bucks' view of Liverpool, 1727.*

in October 1719. The first baptism was that of Ellen, daughter of John and Elizabeth Gill of 'the Woodside', and the first marriage that between Daniel Wilson of Moreton and Jane Stanley, both recorded in August 1721.

Much else can be gleaned from the records. Though small, Birkenhead was clearly not isolated. Apart from the unfortunate persons 'unknown found drowned', there are references to sailors from ships moored in the Sloyne and both 'coach driver' and 'chaise driver' are listed among the father's occupation in the baptismal registers. Clearly there was a lot of through traffic. *The Liverpool Guide* reported that the ferry at Woodside was 'navigated by open boats … for the conveyance of Passengers, Horses, Carriages, Cattle etc.'. The numbers of these can only have increased when the Turnpike Act of 1787 provided for improvements in the road from Chester to Woodside.

38 *The Bucks' view of the Priory, 1727.*

Census, 1801–21			
Year	Birkenhead	Claughton cum Grange	Total of both townships
1801	110	67	177
1811	105	88	193
1821	200	119	319

THE PRICE ESTATE

The first quarter of the 19th century saw the district beginning to change. With inward migration the number of residents almost doubled in two decades.

The turning point had come in 1806 when the lord of the manor, Francis Richard Price, reached his majority and broke the entail on his estates. Birkenhead Hall, the 'genteel house' sometimes confusingly called 'The Priory', had over the years been let to a series of tenants. The Prices themselves lived in a much grander property, 'Bryn-y-pys', near Overton on Dee in Flintshire. Freed of the entail, Price could now dispose of some of his Wirral property and develop his Birkenhead estates.

Several things attracted newcomers to the district. Its sandstone outcrops were a source of good workable stone and its shoreline had the potential to develop as a watering place and, with improvements to the ferry service, it offered an attractive place of residence for the well-to-do of Liverpool who were beginning to move out from the crowded and increasingly congested town centre.

For Birkenhead to become, in effect, Liverpool's 'West End', certain improvements were necessary. The Mersey could experience very high winds and, with its strong currents and a tidal range of over 30 feet, crossing in an open sailing boat was often difficult or dangerous. On 20 March 1753 the *Chester Courant* reported an accident involving the Woodside ferry which, 'by the violence of the wind overset', drowned 11 people. In addition, as Liverpool's trade increased, the numbers of ships on the river soared. Avoiding vessels in full sail must have tested many a ferryman's skills.

39   *Woodside Ferry, 1791, from a painting by W.G. Herdman.*

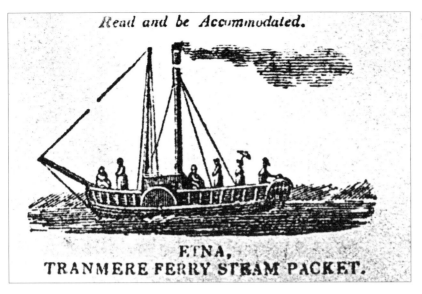

Read and be Accommodated.

ETNA,
TRANMERE FERRY STEAM PACKET.

40 *Advertisement for the Etna, 1817.*

The answer lay with steam navigation. On 5 July 1815 (a month after Waterloo) the *Liverpool Courier* reported 'the arrival of the first Steam Boat ever seen on our River'. This was the paddle steamer *Elizabeth*, built on the Clyde, which had docked in Liverpool on 28 June. Mersey shipbuilders saw the advantage of this new source of power and in the following year several local steamers were launched. Soon a regular steam ferry service was established between Liverpool and a number of Wirral destinations.

One of these was Tranmere. In 1817 the *Etna* or *Aetna*, a double-hulled paddle steamer, very broad in the beam, constructed from two Mersey flats, began a regular half-hour service to and from the Queens Dock:

> This vessel remaining at each side only ten minutes, the certainty with which passengers may calculate upon crossing, at all times of the day, will be an advantage that never yet has been afforded to those whose business or pleasure lead them to cross the river.' (*Liverpool Mercury*)

The breakthrough had been made. With the inauguration of the steam ferry service, albeit to Tranmere, there was only one other obstacle to Birkenhead's expansion. This was the lack of a suitable place of worship. Almost nothing remained of the priory church, and the former Chapter House, which acted as a chapel of ease to Bidston, was, according to the Bishop's Register, 'in such a ruinous and decayed state that divine service could not with safety be performed therein'. The churchyard was also 'too small for the decent interment of the corpses of the deceased Parishioners'.

As part of his plans for Birkenhead, Price agreed to erect a church at his own expense, providing land for both the church and a larger burial ground on a site adjacent to the Priory. In 1818, on the recommendation of the Bishop of Chester, he appointed as architect Thomas Rickman, already making his name in Liverpool for innovative work in cast iron and best known today for dividing Gothic architecture into its four periods or styles. Rickman took a keen personal interest in the project and his diary records several visits to Birkenhead to check on the progress of the work:

> I have had a very satisfactory interview
> with Grindrod the mason.
> 4th September, 1818

The foundation stone for the church was laid on 26 July 1819 by the Rt Hon. Lord Kenyon. Underneath was a 'time capsule', a bottle containing the current coins of George III. In two years the project was complete and on 12 November 1821 the six bells, ordered from William Dobson's foundry in Downham, Norfolk, rang an inaugural peal. Finally, on 17 December, the church was consecrated by the Bishop of Chester and dedicated to St Mary. Its first churchwardens were two hotel keepers, William Mears of the newly opened *Birkenhead Hotel* and William Roberts of Woodside.

Though Price was the driving force, other individuals played a part in the growth of the new settlement. One much quoted 'first inhabitant' was Joseph Harrison. A memoir written by his daughter, Harriet Salt, records him building four cottages in Church Street in 'about 1821' before constructing his riverside villa, 'Mersey Cottage'. Another daughter, Mary, was to marry Thomas Brassey, the assistant of Price's land agent William Lawton and, later, very much involved in the affairs of Birkenhead.

Others who acquired land were two Liverpool stone merchants, Timothy Grindrod, already mentioned, and William Hetherington. In 1813 Hetherington had leased the stone quarry at Flaybrick Hill, gaining permission from Price to run a railway across the fields down to Wallasey Pool. This was Wirral's first 'railway'. It is clearly marked on Greenwood's map of 1819 and thus pre-dates the Storeton tramway by two decades.

41   *Tranmere Ferry, 1844, C.W. Clennell.*

42 *St Mary's Church and churchyard.*

43 *Window tracery, St Mary's church. The church was closed and partially demolished in the 1970s. The east end and tower have been preserved.*

Later they bought more land, including a key site at the southern tip of the headland, where they built the *Birkenhead Hotel*, laying out tea gardens and a bowling green and constructing a small dock and quay. It was from here that the Birkenhead ferry began to run, operated by William Mears. This link between hotel keeper and ferry operator was evidently becoming a pattern. George La French, a former sea captain and at one time licensee of the *Waterloo Hotel* in Church Street, ran the Tranmere ferry for a number of years.

Price was very much a developing landlord and in 1823 he commissioned his land agent, William Lawton, to produce a detailed map of his Birkenhead estates, showing individual holdings, land for sale and properties already sold. The survey, carried out in May of that year, was published in the following January. It recorded in detail the fields, farms and cottages of Birkenhead and Claughton. It also showed the beginnings of a little community, the first few streets, St Mary's Church, the hotels, the ferry landing piers and a number of riverside villas.

WILLIAM LAIRD

Price had been the prime mover in bringing about the first changes to Birkenhead, but the next phase of development is largely attributed to the enterprise of William Laird. Born in Greenock in 1780 and educated in Glasgow, he was the second surviving son of John Laird, a Clyde shipper and owner of the Greenock Ropeworks Company. With his wife Agnes and

44 *The* Birkenhead Hotel, *1828, W.G. Herdman. The hotel's grounds included a tea garden. It was a popular resort for people from Liverpool.*

three small children, Laird had moved to Liverpool in 1810, where he set up in business. Within a few years steam ships arrived on the Mersey, and in 1822 paddle steamers took over the Liverpool-Irish Sea crossing. Laird, who among other things was a proprietor of a steam packet company, was swift to see the opportunities offered by boiler manufacture. To this end he looked for premises to establish a yard.

His choice fell on a block of land adjacent to Wallasey Pool. The decision to move to the Cheshire bank of the Mersey owed much to the situation in Liverpool, where, with the opening of the Prince's Dock in 1821 and plans for further expansion, ship builders and ship repairers were finding themselves increasingly squeezed out from the waterfront. They also faced the threat of rising militancy among the Liverpool workforce, in particular among the journeyman shipwrights. Birkenhead had none of these problems.

The land acquired by Laird is shown on Lawton's map, 54 acres of low-lying fields, formerly part of Bridge End Farm. The works were established at a point known as Vittoria Wharf, where a small, unnamed brook flowed into Wallasey Pool. (Today the site lies at the end of Livingstone Street.) One condition of the sale was that Laird should build 691 yards of new road to replace the section of the old Bidston-Woodside road that ran across his land. The new road became the straight stretch of Cleveland Street.

Laird had no direct experience of iron working, nor a ready supply of iron, so initially the Boiler Yard was run as a joint venture with Daniel and George Horton, of the Ley Ironworks, Brierly Hill, Dudley. The first ledger book is lost but the second, dating from 1827, gives details of their work. Orders for boilers and 'chimneys', presumably funnels, came from several steam packet companies. Boulton and Watt of Soho, Birmingham, the leading boiler manufacturers of the day, passed on work, and a request for retorts was made by the Liverpool Gas Light Company. Laird appears to have been a benevolent employer. As early as 1827 the works had a 'sick club' and Laird was paying Dr William Stevenson 'for medicines and attendance'.

It was a short step from boiler manufacture and ship repairing to actual boat building, and with his eldest son John now a partner William embarked on this new venture. Shipbuilding along traditional lines was already established in the area, St Mary's parish registers showing that among the growing population of the district were ship's carpenters, shipwrights, block makers and sail makers. Now the Lairds were to branch out into the building of iron ships.

On 19 October 1829 the *Albion* newspaper carried the following announcement:

> Launch of Iron Vessels
> On Tuesday 'a somewhat novel sight' was witnessed in Wallasey Pool. An iron vessel has been constructed by Messrs Laird and Co at their extensive steam boiler establishment on the southern side of the Pool.

This was a landmark occasion. The vessel concerned, a small lighter called *Wye*, was the first of hundreds of ships to be launched from the Laird yards. Its construction marked the start of an industry that was to dominate life in Birkenhead for a century and a half.

45   *A portrait of William Laird attributed to T.H. Illidge.*

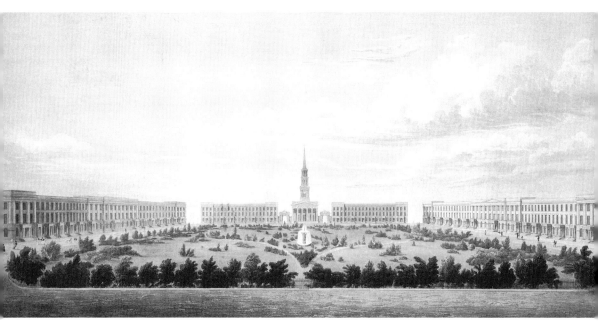

46 *James Gillespie Graham's prospective view of Hamilton Square.*

THE FIRST DOCK SCHEME

William Laird's interests were not confined to his ironworks. He was also involved in much more grandiose plans to build docks in Wallasey Pool. The initial proposal to simply excavate dock basins in the Pool soon mushroomed into the ambitious 'Hilbre Island Scheme'. The civil engineers Thomas Telford, Robert Stephenson and Alexander Nimmo were contracted to undertake a survey.

Their plan was to construct 'two extensive Sea Ports on the Rivers Dee and the Mersey ... with a Floating Harbour or Ship Canal to connect them'. One harbour would be in Wallasey Pool, the other at Hilbre. The two would be linked by a ship canal cut across the low-lying stretches of north Wirral. The scheme had its merits. With access from the Dee, shipping could avoid the difficult approaches to Liverpool. There

would also be ample accommodation for ships of all kinds.

Even before the report was published there was consternation in Liverpool at the prospect of a rival port developing on the Cheshire shore and the consequent loss of revenue from town dues. To prevent this the Corporation had begun to buy land along the river frontage from as early as 1825.

When the plan was finally made public in May 1828, Liverpool Corp-oration offered to purchase further land. While refusing to give Price a firm undertaking, its members implied that they themselves would proceed with at least some part of the proposed scheme. Thus reassured, Price and William Laird, together with Sir John Tobin and others, sold off the remaining Pool frontage to the Corporation. Though set to make a substantial profit on their land sale, their main motive was to ensure that dock building would take place. They were to be disappointed.

The estimated cost of the scheme was enormous, £1,400,948. Even the amended plans only reduced it to £743,713. Faced with these figures the Liverpool Dock Committee made its decision:

> The present dock accommodation together with the new docks now constructing will be amply sufficient to supply the wants of this port for many years to come.

There would be no Birkenhead Docks for nearly 20 years.

The New Town

Parallel with the dock scheme, there were plans for the rest of Birkenhead.

Bounded by the Chester Turnpike, the Woodside to Bidston road and Grange Lane, a tract of land was waiting to be developed.

In Mortimer we read that

> In 1824, the late Mr William Laird, Esq. ... purchased a large quantity of land about the centre of the town, with the intention of erecting upon it buildings in a style of magnificence unsurpassed in this part of the kingdom. The execution of his plans was confided to Mr Gillespie Graham, of Edinburgh, from whose designs Hamilton Square and the Streets immediately adjacent were laid out.

Mortimer would seem to be mistaken in suggesting that Laird purchased a large quantity of land. The Land

47   *Activity on the waterfront. The Birkenhead Ferry slipway, with the* Birkenhead Hotel *in the background.*

Tax returns for the period show that, following the building of his church, a wide range of individuals bought land from Price, either for their own use or as an investment. Price himself retained a proportion of his estate, also intent on profit.

Laird's involvement was, however, crucial, for it can have been only he who persuaded James Gillespie Graham, the leading Scottish architect of the day, to design the elevations and street plan for the new part of the town. That an architect of such eminence should accept this, his only English commission, has always been a puzzle. Birkenhead was as yet little more than an idea. The explanation must surely lie in the long-established links between the Laird family and Gillespie Graham, dating from the start of the century.

As early as 1800, when just plain James Gillespie, he had engaged John Laird, William's father, to ship to Skye various items needed for work on Lord Macdonald's estates. This connection between the architect and the Lairds continued for over two decades. Significantly, among the items carried on a Laird ship in 1813 were Gillespie's plans for a new town at Kyleakin.

Though little was eventually built at Kyleakin, a memory of the scheme must have stayed with the Lairds. In the meantime Gillespie had risen in reputation. Marrying an heiress, he had taken her name, Graham. By 1822 he was styling himself 'Architect to His Majesty in Scotland' and had just completed preparing plans for his major work, the planning of part of Edinburgh's New Town.

It is often claimed that it was on the basis of his work in Edinburgh that Gillespie Graham won the commission to plan Birkenhead, though at this stage his work had scarcely begun. More likely it was as a favour to an old acquaintance that he agreed to prepare the Birkenhead plan. The effort involved may not have been great. Armed with a copy of Lawton's survey, he had no need to visit Wirral for himself. Furthermore, the close resemblance between properties in Hamilton Square and the design of some of his Edinburgh houses suggests that, never the most scrupulous of individuals and a past master at reusing drawings, he did not even produce new house designs but simply recycled existing plans.

One important thing for which Gillespie Graham can, however, be justly credited was the scheme adopted for the development of Hamilton Square. Following a procedure similar to that obtaining in Edinburgh, the design of all properties was governed by a single plan, though individual purchasers were responsible for engaging builders and putting the plan into effect. The cost of everything, houses, stables, boundary walls, railings and so on, was borne by those for whom the houses were built or by speculative builders. No costs would accrue to Price, Laird or Gillespie Graham himself.

With the new town off the drawing board, all seemed set fair for the future predicted in the *Liverpool Mercury* of 1828: Birkenhead 'may, at no very distant period, become of considerable importance, if not as a watering place, at least as a favourite sojourn of the merchants of Liverpool'.

6

Improvement—'The Magic Wand'

THE NEW COMMUNITY

The failure of its dock scheme, though disappointing, was not a sufficient set-back to halt the rise of Birkenhead. The first Rate Book, dated 1829 and compiled by William Laird and Thomas Brassey acting as overseers, gives a snap-shot of the growing settlement. There were nine streets, with '237 dwelling houses, two hotels, three inns, eleven houses and shops, two ferries, four yards and workshops and 53 assessments on farms and land'.

The census of 1831 provides exact population figures. In 10 years numbers in Birkenhead and Claughton had risen from 319 to 2,793. Together the two townships now formed the largest settlement in Wirral, outstripping Neston and even exceeding the combined populations of Wallasey, Liscard, Poulton and Seacombe (2,727).

To accommodate these growing numbers a Bill went before Parliament in 1832 for the enlargement of St Mary's Church. What Pevsner describes as two 'monstrous transepts' were added to Rickman's elegant structure. Five years later work started on a second Anglican church, Holy Trinity, Price Street. Idiosyncratic in style, it was covered with grotesque heads and described in the

journal *The Ecclesiologist* as 'so execrable as not to be worth criticism'. It opened in 1840, standing at first almost alone among former fields, and became a parish church in its own right in 1841.

Elsewhere, other places of worship were appearing. In 1830 the Brunswick Wesleyan Methodist Chapel opened in Price Street, paid for by public subscription. On 14 September 1835 the foundation stone of St Werburgh's Catholic Chapel in Grange Lane was laid by the Rev. Thomas Youens DD. Intended 'for the accommodation of worshippers and visitors in this beautiful place', it was built to the design of M.E. Hatfield and opened in 1837. Two years later came the Baptist Union Chapel on the corner of Argyle Street. In the same year the foundation stone of St Andrew's Presbyterian Church was laid in Conway Street. Known as the 'Scotch Kirk', it was the main place of worship for the strong Scottish community present in the town.

Linked to the various churches and chapels were schoolrooms, some intended primarily for Sunday Schools, but many serving as weekday classrooms as well. The earliest of these was attached to St Mary's and is probably the 'Birkenhead School' mentioned in the Land Tax

48   *St Werburgh's Church, one of the first places of worship in Birkenhead.*

return for 1825. Certainly its long-serving schoolmaster, George Platt, was in post by 1829. Such denominational schools represented the first attempt to bring an elementary education to the ordinary children of Birkenhead. For those families who could afford them, a number of private establishments existed that catered both for day scholars and boarders. Among these was the small school in Brandon Street attended by the seven-year-old Henry Aspinall, and the girls' school run by a Miss Koster in the former Hall.

An institution of another sort was the Petty Sessions Court, established in the town in 1832. Here the Wirral magistrates dealt with a succession of minor offences: brawling outside a public house, singing and dancing after hours, drunkenness, using abusive language, disturbing the neighbours, stealing apples and even playing dominoes for a glass of ale. Traffic regulations were also enforced.

Informers, stationed on the turnpike, regularly reported on coaches carrying more passengers than their licences permitted.

As the population swelled, the whole district took on a more urban character. West of the original nucleus, the formal gridiron plan of roads was being laid out and the surrounding fields divided into lots and fenced off. The fate of the farm tenants is not recorded but the grumbles of a disgruntled 'Pedestrian' foreshadow the sentiments of later rambling enthusiasts:

> Every vestige of the pleasant footpaths, through the fields ... have, within a few days, vanished! And clay ditches, with rails upon them, oppose your progress at every fifty or sixty yards. The field-road leading from the back of Woodside towards Oxton, which has existed from time immemorial, has shared the general fate; no more rural walks through Birkenhead.

To regulate and pay for these changes there was a clear need to improve the machinery of local government. To this end, F.R. Price, as the principal landowner, and the majority of the freeholders petitioned Parliament for an Improvement Bill. Their case was based on the rapid growth of the town.

> Whereas ... Birkenhead ... being situated on the Banks of the River Mersey opposite the Town of Liverpool, is a Place of great Resort and hath a considerable Population, which is greatly increasing.

Their plea was heard and for the next forty years, until 1877, the civic administration of Birkenhead would be in the hands of Improvement Commissioners.

THE BIRKENHEAD IMPROVEMENT COMMISSIONERS

On 10 June 1833 William IV gave royal assent to the first Birkenhead Improvement Act.

Its main concerns were public health and public order and it charged the new authority with the

> paving, lighting, watching, cleansing and otherwise improving the Township or Chapelry of Birkenhead and for regulating the Police thereof and for establishing a Market.

It also laid down the composition of the original Improvement Commission. This was to include the Mayor and Bailiffs of Liverpool, four of its junior aldermen and 60 named local gentry, merchants and tradesmen, among whom were Francis Richard Price, Thomas Brassey and both William and John Laird. It was

49 *Before the coming of the railway, Birkenhead was served by a regular coach service running between Chester and the* Woodside Hotel. *The stream of traffic increased with the building of a causeway across Tranmere Pool.*

an unwieldy body and in 1838 a second Act reduced its size to more manageable proportions. It had the power to levy a rate and to borrow money for the physical improvement of the town. Its first meeting was in the recently erected Magistrates' Rooms on 25 June 1833, the third Tuesday after the passing of the Act.

In the 1830s the prevention of crime was very much on people's minds so one of the first actions of the new

Commissioners was to appoint James Booth, already acting as the police constable for the magistrates, to serve as police officer to the township as well. Subsequently they also employed two watchmen to be on duty at night and to be responsible for lighting the town's lamps. In addition the three men were to operate a fire engine, if and when required. As the number of lamps increased, a separate lamplighter was engaged, while two further constables were appointed to assist Booth with police duties during the day.

The roads also needed attention. The turnpike from Chester, the main route for coach traffic, was the responsibility of a turnpike trust, but the district's other roads the Commissioners found in 'a dangerous state', as their first Minute Book records:

50 *Footscrapers, like the ones in Hamilton Square, were very necessary before the Commissioners improved the roads.*

Notice be given to Mr T. Brassey that the footpath in Chester St be put into a proper state for the public safety to the satisfaction of the road committee.'

In addition, new roads had to be laid out and properly surfaced:

Mr Brassey to be written to, to complete Hamilton street, opposite to Mr Price's land.

Cleansing was also a concern. In contrast to the well-designed plan of the new town, the area round the Priory had developed in a most unregulated way. Stretching back from the main streets were 'courts', narrow alleyways lacking light and ventilation and with several families sharing a privy and midden. There were no drains, stagnant water accumulated in pits and watercourses and conditions in many streets were described as 'offensive'. Straying pigs and cattle wandered loose and butchers and 'hawkers' sold food from open carts. Disease was rife and epidemics were an ever-present threat.

One solution was sanitation. An extensive network of drains and sewers was constructed, flowing directly into Tranmere and Wallasey Pools and into the Mersey itself. To some extent the exercise was futile as the Commissioners lacked the powers to compel house builders and owners to link their properties to the system. Numerous households still relied on open cess pits, the effluent from which often seeped into nearby pumps and wells. The consequence was inevitable and cholera, which had broken out in Liverpool in 1832, crossed the Mersey in the summer of 1834 and by August was 'raging' in the overcrowded households of Back Chester Street and

51 *The 1833 Improvement Act placed the future of Birkenhead in the hands of Improvement Commissioners.*

ANNO TERTIO

GULIELMI IV. REGIS.

****

Cap. lxviii.

An Act for paving, lighting, watching, cleansing, and otherwise improving the Township or Chapelry of *Birkenhead* in the County Palatine of *Chester*, and for regulating the Police thereof, and for establishing a Market within the said Township. [10th *June* 1833.]

WHEREAS the Township or Chapelry of *Birkenhead* in the County of *Chester*, being situated on the Banks of the River *Mersey* opposite the Town of *Liverpool*, is a Place of great Resort and hath a considerable Population, which is rapidly increasing: And whereas there is no established Market within the said Township: And whereas *Francis Richard Price* Esquire, Lord of the Manor of *Birkenhead*, claims to be seised of or entitled to, in Fee Simple, a Piece or Parcel of Ground within the said Township well calculated for the Area or Site of a Market, which he is willing to give up to the Inhabitants of the said Township to be used as a Market for the Sale of Provisions and other Articles: And whereas the Roads, Streets, Lanes, and other public Passages and Places within the said Township are not properly paved, lighted, watched, and cleansed, and are subject to various Nuisances, Annoyances, and Obstructions, and it would be of great Benefit and Advantage to the Inhabitants of the said Township, and to all Persons resorting thereto, if the said Road, Streets, Lanes, and other public Passages and Places were properly paved, lighted, watched, and cleansed, and freed from all Nuisances, Annoyances, and Obstructions, and if an effective Police were established in the said Township; but the several

[*Local*.] 17 *K* beneficia.

its adjoining courts. Lacking any real understanding of how cholera was transmitted, the authorities could only resort to ordering pits and channels to be washed out with lime water, and rounding up stray pigs to be placed in the pinfold.

To raise revenue to supplement the rates the Commissioners were to establish a market. The right to hold one was traditionally the lord of the manor's but Price relinquished his rights to the commissioners and, in addition, donated a plot of land on the corner of Hamilton Street and Market Street on which a suitable building could be erected. The architect chosen for the project was Clark Rampling and he was asked to produce plans for a Market Hall, Lock Up and Civic Offices.

The new building was to be one of substance. The front, in Greek Revival

52   *Old Market and Town Hall.*

style, was constructed of Storeton stone, the rest of stone from the Flaybrick quarries. Inside, the Magistrates' Room would be fitted with marble chimney pieces and there was to be a water closet, flushed with water collected from the roof. A large lead-lined cistern, eight feet across, would store water for general use.

The Market itself would have 25 shops and separate stalls for fruit, vegetables, game and meat, with special stone slabs provided for the fishmongers. On vacant ground to the rear, space was set aside for the sale of hay, straw and grass. (With the horse still the main means of transport, a haymarket was an important feature of any town.)

The contract for the Market went to a local builder, Walter Walker. By June 1835 the work was almost complete and a Market Committee was set up to supervise its affairs. To succeed, the enterprise needed to attract both stallholders and customers, and placards and handbills were printed announcing the twice-weekly market days, Wednesday and Saturday, with notices placed in the Liverpool and Chester papers. On 11 July the market opened for the first time, announced by the ringing of a bell.

In addition to the Market, the Commissioners established a Fair with the intention of attracting custom from the surrounding rural areas. The Fair was advertised in papers as far flung as the *Carlisle Packet*, the *Bolton Chronicle* and the *Dublin Evening Post*.

> Birkenhead, opposite Liverpool— Cattle & Cheese Fairs
>
> Fairs for the sale of Horned Cattle, Sheep, Horses, Cheese, Hops etc. And will be holden at Birkenhead in the west of Chester on Tuesday the 8th day of October 1839, Tuesday the 24th of April and Thursday the 3rd day of July 1840.

THE FERRY AND THE RAILWAY

The success of the Market and Fair and indeed of the town as a whole depended on a reliable ferry service across the Mersey. At the time three ferries served the locality: the Woodside ferry and the paddle-steamers, the latter running from the slipway attached to the *Birkenhead Hotel* and from Tranmere. The rights to the Woodside ferry belonged to Francis Price and were leased by him to Hugh Williams. In the autumn of 1834 the Commissioners approached Price requesting more regular sailings. They themselves had no authority to run a ferry. Instead a group of local businessmen, including John Laird and William Jackson, formed the Woodside, North Birkenhead and Liverpool Steam Ferry Company and took over the ferry lease. Sailings were now assured and a contract was agreed with the Postmaster General to continue to carry the mail.

Parallel with improvements in the ferry service came plans for a railway. The little tramway which ran from Flaybrick quarry down to Wallasey Pool showed how easily bulky goods could be carried by rail, while the opening of the Liverpool to Manchester railway in 1830 offered further proof

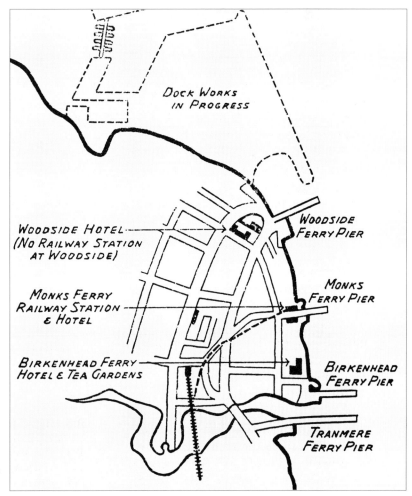

53 *Map showing route of the railway.*

of the importance of rail to passengers. Within a few weeks of the official opening of the L&M, plans were put forward to provide a rail link between Chester and Liverpool, terminating at Birkenhead.

Nothing came of these first schemes until 1836 when interest revived. In 1837 two rival bills were placed before Parliament, which in a surprising move appointed arbitrators to choose between the competing proposals. Mainly on the basis of his much lower estimate, their choice fell on the scheme drawn up by George Stephenson for the Chester and Birkenhead Railway Company, among whose shareholders were William and John Somerville Jackson, John Laird and Thomas Brassey. Stephenson's planned route would have finished at Woodside but, anxious not to favour

one ferry company above another, Parliament insisted that the line terminate at Grange Lane. The first sod was cut in May 1838 and in two years a single track line was complete. On 22 September 1840 came the official opening. Numerous dignitaries were in attendance when 'a train of enormous length' steamed out of the station, pulled by the two engines, *Touchstone* and *Zillah*, the event being marked by the firing of cannon.

At first the company ran five trains a day, with an additional 'market train' from Chester on Wednesdays and Saturdays. The service was swift and reliable, but the fares compared unfavourably with those charged by coach operators. Many travellers continued to use the roads and the company was slow to make a profit. Only when fares were

54   *Monks Ferry in 1844, looking down Ivy Street, towards the slip. C.W.Clennell.*

55 *Hamilton Square, looking west down Cleveland Street. Both William Jackson and his brother, John Somerville Jackson, occupied houses in the Square, before moving to larger homes.*

reduced did travel by rail effectively replace the stagecoach. Cost apart, a difficulty facing rail travellers was getting between Grange Lane and Woodside. To overcome this, an omnibus service was provided free of charge to first- and second-class passengers; third-class passengers were presumably expected to make their own way.

There were restrictions on extending the line to Woodside unless links were provided to the other two ferries, but a new ferry would not be limited by the 1837 legislation. Perhaps appreciative of this loophole, two of the railway shareholders, Richard and James Bryans, had built a hotel and slipway at Ivy Rock, some 400 yards south of Woodside, and began to run a service from there which they named the Monks' Ferry. The legality of their actions was challenged in the courts and in February 1840 they were forced to stop operating.

The saga did not end there. In 1838 the railway company had acquired control of the Woodside Ferry Company. It now stepped in to purchase the Monks' Ferry. When, after a couple of years, neither enterprise proved profitable it offered them both to the Commissioners. In return it sought permission to cut a tunnel from Grange Lane down to the Monks' Ferry slip. After protracted negotiations and the necessary Acts of Parliament, both ferries became the property of the town and the railway was extended to the shore.

WILLIAM JACKSON

One leading light in the affairs of the ferry and railway was William Jackson, a Liverpool merchant who had made his fortune trading with Africa. Not yet 40, he had retired from business and now set his entrepreneurial sights on Birkenhead. His first venture was in

56   *Portrait of William Jackson.*

57   *The grave of William Jackson in Flaybrick cemetery.*

gas. The town's first street lamps, fixed to iron posts, burned whale or seal oil. Following the example of Liverpool, already partially lighted by gas, the Commissioners soon considered it as an alternative. They could have established their own 'manufactory' but instead decided to rely on private enterprise. Several tenders were considered, and in 1840 the contract was awarded to Jackson, by now one of the town's major landowners and, until only a short time before, a Commissioner. Jackson had already purchased suitable land, close to the margins of Tranmere Pool. In selecting this site, still visible at the bottom of Jackson Street, he was fully aware of its advantages. The new railway line ran immediately to

the east and the works were therefore ideally placed to receive supplies of coal by rail.

The Improvement Act of 1838 had empowered the Commissioners to construct a waterworks, but nothing had been done. Residents still relied on water supplies drawn from pumps and shallow wells or, in the poorer parts of the town, on rainwater collected in butts. Little had changed in the 200 years since the death of William Chantrell of Noctorum, who in the inventory of his personal estate, dated 1648, had one 'stone cistern'.

Not content with acquiring the contract for supplying gas, William Jackson, together with his brother John Somerville Jackson and Joseph Mallaby,

103.

ANNO QUARTO & QUINTO

VICTORIÆ REGINÆ.

58 *The Gas and Waterworks Act of 1841.*

✳✳

Cap. lxii.

An Act for supplying *Birkenhead* and other Townships in the Hundred of *Wirrall* in the County of
Chester with Gas, and for supplying *Birkenhead*
aforesaid with Water.   [21st *June* 1841.]

WHEREAS the Townships of *Birkenhead, Tranmere, Lower
Bebington, Higher Bebington, Bromborough, Great Neston,
Little Neston, Poulton cum Spittle, Thornton, Hough, Upton,
Bidston, Oxton, Claughton, Prenton, Poulton cum Seacombe, Liscard,*
and *Wallasey,* in the County of *Chester,* are very populous and increasing in Population, and it would be a Source of great Advantage
to the Inhabitants thereof if the said Townships were lighted with
Gas; and the Inhabitants of the said Township of *Birkenhead* would
be also much benefited by a more constant and regular Supply of
Water than they now enjoy: And whereas the several Persons herein-
after mentioned, together with others, are willing, at their own Ex-
pence, to carry into effect the beneficial Objects aforesaid: May it
therefore please Your Majesty that it may be enacted; and be it
enacted by the Queen's most Excellent Majesty, by and with the
Advice and Consent of the Lords Spiritual and Temporal, and Com-
mons, in this present Parliament assembled, and by the Authority
of the same, That *William Jackson, John Somerville Jackson, Gilbert*

[*Local.*]   14 *I*   *Henry*

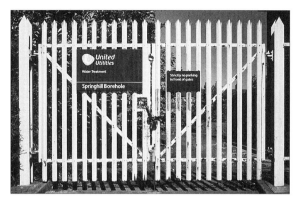

59 *The site of the original Spring Hill waterworks on Balls Road.*

the Law Clerk, placed a private bill before Parliament for the right to supply the town with water. There was an element of sharp practice involved and the Commissioners appeared unaware of the scheme until it was too late. In June 1841 Parliament gave approval to

> An Act for supplying Birkenhead and other Townships in the Hundred of Wirral in the county of Chester with Gas, and for supplying Birkenhead aforesaid with Water.

The Commissioners had thus let the right to provide both gas and water pass into private hands.

Jackson's waterworks were built on the aptly named Spring Hill on what is now Balls Road. They stood some 100 feet above sea level, on the higher ground above the town. A boring was sunk through the sandstone to a depth of some 300 feet and a pumping engine installed to draw up the water. The undertaking, which included a reservoir, was completed in 1843. As Mortimer, a protégé of Jackson, commented, 'The works, from their elevation and ornamental chimney, form a very

conspicuous object.' What he failed to mention was that the supply was often intermittent and even non-existent for two or three days a week. Worse still, numerous households, especially in the poorer parts of the town, still relied on cisterns or pumps or had no water at all. Eventually further boreholes were sunk and in 1858 the works were taken over by the Improvement Commissioners.

THE CARE OF THE POOR

With so much of the town so recently built it might have been expected that Birkenhead would escape the problems of poverty and squalor which affected Liverpool across the water, but this was not always the case. The Commissioners' task was to improve the physical environment but the relief of the poor was beyond their remit. It was the overseers of the poor who collected the local poor rate and distributed it to the needy. The rise in expenditure on the poor was a national concern. In Wirral as a whole the average cost of poor relief was only 18d. per head but it was much higher in the increasingly urban townships round Birkenhead. Something had to be done.

In September 1834 the Birkenhead Overseer wrote to the newly appointed Poor Law Commissioners explaining that the township was going through 'hard times'. Expenditure on a work-house would be justified if it could offer a long-term solution to the rising cost of poor relief. The Commissioners agreed and Birkenhead, together with all the other Wirral parishes, was grouped into the Wirral Poor Law Union in 1836. Land for a workhouse was acquired at Clatterbridge, five miles from Birk-enhead and at a central point in the peninsula.

1836—Extract from Appendix to Second Annual Report of Poor Law Commissioners				
Parish	Population in 1831	Expenditure on Poor Average for years 1833–1835	Expenditure per head of Population	Number of Guardians
Birkenhead	2,569	£321	2/6d	2
Tranmere	1,168	£199	3/4d	1
Bidston with Ford	251	£60	4/10d	1
Claughton cum Grange	224	£18	1/1d	1
Oxton	234	£15	10d	1
Noctorum	28	No poor	0d	1

On 17 May 1836 the Guardians of the new Wirral Poor Law Union met for the first time in the Magistrates' Room in Birkenhead. Birkenhead was represented by William Ravenscroft and William Jackson, Tranmere by George Taylor and Oxton by George King. Until the workhouse was ready they and the other Guardians met to award outdoor relief, always anxious to discourage the able-bodied pauper.

Sometimes the merits of a case were clear:

> Birkenhead: Jane Parry—her child Jane dead—ordered 12/6 for funeral.
>
> Oxton: Thomas Kingsley ... 2/- per week, blind and unable to earn his living.
>
> Claughton cum Grange: Catherine Hill—imbecile and ill, an additional 1/-.
>
> Tranmere: Ann Bilsbarrow, pauper, having broken her arm, ordered 6d. per week additional.

Orphaned and abandoned children were often a problem:

> Noctorum: A deserted infant left by its mother in a field in the occupation of Mr Jackson the overseer and sent by him to the Birkenhead Bridewell, where it has been nursed by Mrs Booth since Friday last, 3/6 per week for nurse, 10/- for clothing, 10/- expenses.

The needs of two Tranmere brothers came up with regularity:

> 26 September 1836: John and Hugh Hughes—clothing.
>
> 6 September 1837: John and Hugh Hughes—a cap each.
>
> 20 September 1837: John Hughes, an orphan—a pair of trowsers not exceed'g 4/-.
>
> 22 November 1837: John Hughes requires a pair of clogs.
>
> 6 December 1837: Hugh Hughes ordered a pair of clogs.

Even when Clatterbridge opened, a decision was made to continue their outdoor relief:

21 March 1838: John and Hugh
Hughes in want of clothing,
ordered 26/- as a loan to be
stopped out of pay, this to be
raised from 1/6 to 1/9.

The brothers were fortunate. For those
less lucky there would be no more
outdoor assistance. Help from now on
would be conditional on going into
the workhouse.

'A PLEASANT PLACE TO LIVE'

Poverty was one side of the picture.
For the most part the new town was
flourishing and was clearly a pleasant
place to live. Henry Aspinall, born
in 1824, described the shore of his
boyhood:

The Woodside beach, north of
the slip, was composed of hard
dry sand, well suited for bathing.
Many visitors from Liverpool and
the country round come for the
bathing season. The water was
always clear and the bathing
machines were well patronised.
Donkeys were on hire and the
merriment ran high.

A contemporary report praised
Birkenhead for its 'salubrity' and
included the often quoted remark
that Liverpool doctors recommended
'their patients to avail themselves of
its benefits'.

But it was not just visitors who came
for the 'pureness of the air'. With a
regular ferry service across the Mersey,
numerous Liverpool merchants were
now making Birkenhead their home.
By the end of its first decade the little
town for which the Commissioners had
taken responsibility in 1833 had more
than quadrupled in size. It seemed on its
way to becoming a place 'of considerable
importance'.

7

The Merchants' Pride—
Early Victorian Birkenhead

THE BOOM YEARS

The arrival of the railway in 1840 gave a new dimension to Birkenhead's development. It now had links via Chester to the south, and by 1846 was connected to the coalfields of North Wales. In time it would become an important terminus, with several stations and extensive areas within the town given over to railway sidings.

Railway construction required a huge labour force. At its peak, in October 1839, some 2,030 men were working on the line, among them many Irish navvies. When fighting broke out at Childer Thornton between English and Irish labourers the police were summoned from Birkenhead. So great was the disorder that the violence was only controlled when additional help was sought from the militia. This particular clash was probably economic in origin but it presaged a number of unhappy episodes of sectarian rivalry.

It was not just the railway that brought workers to the district. House and road building, the gas- and water-works, the brickfields, the shipyards and the boiler works all required labour, while at the other end of the social scale the 'salubrity' of the area continued to attract Liverpool merchants. By 1841 Birkenhead was largely a town of incomers. From a total population of 8,223, including a further 240 in Claughton, only one third had been born in Cheshire, a pattern reflected in Wirral as a whole. Of the 33,678 inhabitants of the Hundred, 19,184 were natives of Cheshire, 11,220 came from other parts of England, 1,981 were Irish, 826 were Scottish, 131 were born abroad and the birthplace of 336 was 'unknown'. Women outnumbered men, a reflection in part of the high demand for those described by the census as 'female servants'.

This explosion in population prompted an application to Parliament for yet another Improvement Act. This authorised the extension of Birkenhead's boundaries to include the townships of Claughton-cum-Grange and those parts of Oxton into which it was already spreading. The Commissioners were given additional borrowing rights and the power to purchase land for improvements and for the formation of a park. They were also permitted to set up a Health Committee, appoint a Surveyor and exercise some control over housing and sanitation.

THE NEW MARKET HALL

By 1843 the original Market no longer met 'the increased wants' of the growing

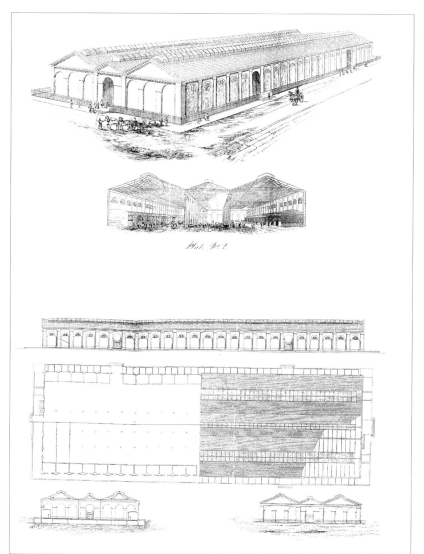

town. Spurred on by their new borrowing powers, the Commissioners embarked on a grandiose scheme to build a much larger Market Hall, giving the contract to the iron founders Fox, Henderson and Co. who later became famous for their work on the Crystal Palace. The new structure, 430 feet long and 131 feet wide, was built on the land acquired between Hamilton and Albion Street. It housed 42 shops and some 80 stalls and was widely promoted as being larger than any of Liverpool's covered markets, with the exception of St John's. Constructed of brick, glass and iron, it had a wrought-iron roof supported by cast-iron columns, and each shop was protected by wrought-iron shutters. Underneath were brick arched storage vaults and in the market itself were two ornamental fountains. The whole was designed to be totally fireproof but, having survived the Blitz, when many local residents took shelter in its vaults, it was badly damaged by fire in 1974 and subsequently replaced.

Apart from running the Market itself, its Committee was responsible for letting rooms in the Town Hall. The list of bookings gives a glimpse of the informal side of town life. Among those requesting rooms were some of the town's smaller religious congregations, the Welsh Calvinistic Methodists, the Scotch Secession Church and the Baptists. Lectures, concerts, meetings and sales of work were also organised by groups as varied as the Total Abstinence Society, the Dispensary Committee, the Mechanics' Institute, the Chartists' Cooperative Land Company, the Hospital Committee and the Ladies Clothing Society. An application from a 'dancing academy' was at first turned down.

THE PARK

Birkenhead is justly proud of its pioneering position in the history of public parks. Though the Town Moor in Preston had been laid out as a park in 1833 and Derby Arboretum, opened in 1840, was the gift of Joseph Strutt, Birkenhead boasts the first municipal park provided entirely out of public funds. Its influence was far reaching. In the 1850s it even attracted a visit from the American 'father of landscape architecture', Frederick Law Olmsted, who with Calvert Vaux went on to create Central Park, New York.

The benefit of a park to a growing town had already been recognised in the report of a Parliamentary Select Committee on Public Walks:

61   *Interior of Market Hall.*

> With rapidly increasing Population, lodged for the most part in narrow courts and confined streets, the means of occasional exercise and recreation in the fresh air are everyday lessened, as inclosures take place and buildings spread themselves on every side.

This certainly applied to Birkenhead, where the only open space designated in its gridiron plan was Hamilton Square, whose gardens were to remain in private hands until 1903. As the local press pointed out,

> Brick and mortar are there so fast taking the place of green fields and sooty vapours are so thickly mingling with the fragrant breezes that … Birkenhead will soon no longer be in the country. It is therefore good policy to provide a healthy and agreeable place of resort to secure the permanent benefits of pure air and exercise, at a moderate distance from the town, while this can be done at a comparatively trifling cost. (*Liverpool Courier*, 10 August 1842)

Isaac Holmes, a Liverpool representative on the Improvement Commission, first proposed a 'place of resort' in 1841, and parliamentary approval came with the Improvement Act of 1843. In advance of the scheme various individuals, including William Jackson, John Laird and Thomas Brassey, had already bought land from Price in the area where the park was proposed. That many of them gained from the subsequent resale of this land is not to their credit.

In August 1843 the Commissioners engaged Joseph Paxton, Superintendent of the Duke of Devonshire's gardens at Chatsworth, to design the park. The year before he had been commissioned by Richard Vaughan Yates to lay out the private development of Princes Park, Liverpool; in Birkenhead he was to work on the first municipal park in the world.

The site was not promising. Paxton described its 226 acres as 'not a very good situation' but he saw that the effective use of the land could only rebound to his credit. His plans included all the features then thought necessary for a park: ornamental lakes, internal carriage drives, winding paths, areas of close planting and stretches of open grassland, the whole designed to have all the attributes of a romantic rural landscape.

The venture was expensive, but essential to the successful funding of the park was the sale of house plots within its perimeter. Here the villas and terraces had to conform to a strict set of design criteria, something sadly not required of later development.

Though the design of the park was Paxton's own, its implementation was left to Edward Kemp, a landscape gardener who had trained under Paxton at Chatsworth. Kemp was subsequently appointed Park Superintendent, living in the Italian Lodge until 1860. Later he was made responsible for the design and laying out of the cemetery at Flaybrick.

Another of Paxton's protégés, John Robertson, is credited with the design of the lodges. He had been Paxton's architectural assistant and is best known for his designs for Edensor, a model village on the Chatsworth estate. Robertson's lodges are small and picturesque and reflect the medley of styles popular at the time, Gothic, Italianate, Greek Revival and Castellated.

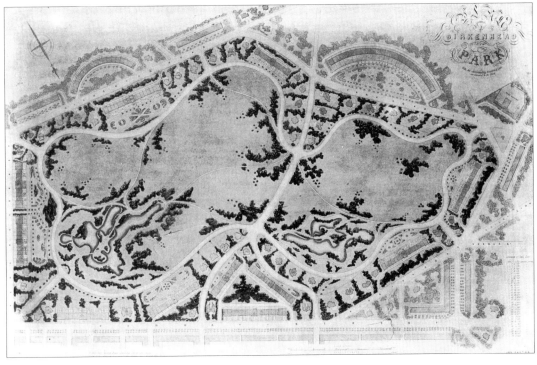

62   *Plan of the park, drawn by John Robertson to a design by Joseph Paxton.*

Crucial to the park design were the two lakes. These served a dual function. Their provision aided the drainage of the site, much of which had been water meadow, while material excavated from the lakes was available for landscaping. Equally importantly, they served an aesthetic purpose. Together they made up eight acres of water, but with their deliberately sinuous outline and the islands at their centre, they had the appearance of much larger bodies of water.

Kemp was essentially a landscape designer so a local architect, Lewis Hornblower, still in his early twenties, was engaged to produce plans for the park's structural features: the Boathouse, the Swiss Bridge, the Cast Iron Bridge, the gate piers and the railings. Hornblower also produced designs for the main gate but these were rejected by Paxton as too grandiose and out of keeping

with the rest of the park. The modified Grand Entrance is still imposing, so it is difficult to imagine how it might have looked had Hornblower had his way. His early experience in Birkenhead served him well, for later, in co-operation with Edouard André, Hornblower went on to produce the winning design for Liverpool's Sefton Park.

The aim of Birkenhead Park was provision for all. In 1846, even before the official opening, a cricket club was formed and a pitch established in the lower park. Individual entrepreneurs provided other facilities: a camera obscura, a Refreshment Salon and an aerial walkway across the lower lake (although this was to collapse within a few years and the experiment was never repeated).

In keeping with its aim, the park's opening day was celebrated with a

63   *View of the park bandstand and boathouse, 1847.*

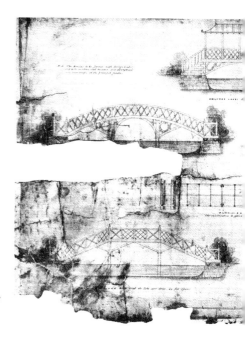

64   *Hornblower's designs for features in the park. The wear and tear to the plans suggests they were used on site.*

65   *The Grand Entrance to the park at its official opening, 5 April 1847.*

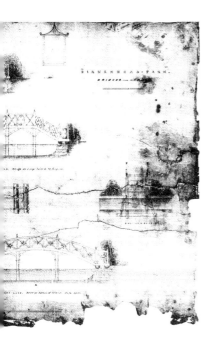

66 *Aerial view of the park, looking to the south-west. The railway can be seen emerging from the tunnel at Park Station on the right-hand side of the photograph.*

67 *Central Park, New York in winter. The lake resembles those in Birkenhead.*

68   *'Laying the Foundation Stone of Birkenhead Docks', H.F. Oakes, 1844.*

programme of 'Rural Sports'. Only one event seems to have disturbed the local press:

> RACE FOR WOMEN OF ALL AGES. The less said about this race the better, our notions of what females ought to do not embracing running races.'

The importance of the park persists. In 1977 it was made a Conservation Area and in 1995 designated a Grade 1 Listed Landscape. Finally, at the millennium, a major restoration programme was begun, a key feature being the provision of a new pavilion and the restoration of the Boathouse and the Swiss Bridge.

THE DOCKS
Parallel with the creation of the park came a renewal of interest in the dock scheme. The arrival of the railway in 1840 had made possible the overland transportation of heavy or bulky goods, to and from Birkenhead. At the same time Liverpool Corporation, which had allowed much of the land it had acquired in 1828 to lie idle, was now anxious to capitalise on its value and use the proceeds to reduce the charges it imposed on its ratepayers.

Thus, on 30 October 1843, Liverpool Council, apparently blind to what was planned, agreed to sell the very land it had purchased 15 years earlier in order to thwart the original dock scheme. Land along the waterfront was offered in lots and some 200,000 square yards sold off for £120,000 on 75-year leases. The purchasers included John Laird, William Potter, William Jackson and William Cole. Laird, who since the death of his father was now in sole charge of the ironworks, acquired about a quarter of the land, 48,000 square yards, bought at 10s. a square yard.

When, on 7 November, the dock scheme was made public to the Improvement Commissioners, Liverpool Corporation appears to have been taken completely by surprise. It seemed astonished to learn that the civil engineer J.M. Rendell had already drawn up plans and the Board of the Admiralty given approval for the enclosure of Wallasey Pool. Despite spirited opposition from Liverpool, Parliament's consent was granted for the first Birkenhead Dock Bill (7 & 8 Victoria, c.79, 1844) on 19 July 1844. As the historian Picton tartly remarked, the Corporation had 'attempted to gather wool ... and certainly come home shorn'.

On 23 October 1844 Sir Philip Egerton, MP for Cheshire County, laid the foundation stone of the Docks, the ceremony being performed with a silver trowel. Beneath the stone had been placed a time capsule: a glass bottle containing a Liverpool newspaper, plans of the works and a coin of the day. The occasion was one of huge celebration and crowds gathered from both sides of the Mersey. In Birkenhead working men had been given a paid holiday and many of them processed through Hamilton Square under a triumphal arch of laurel. Children, too, were involved and given gifts of fruit and buns. On that bright autumn day, as the flags flew and the bands played, it must have seemed that the future of Birkenhead was secure.

WORKERS' HOUSING AND VILLA ESTATES

The labour force required to build the Docks was huge, numbering at one stage some fifteen hundred men. Anticipating a need for housing, the dock company directors commissioned a local architect, Charles Evans Lang, to design what were to be some of the first artisan 'flats' in England. On 3 May 1845 the *Liverpool Journal* presented its subscribers with a supplement containing plans and elevations of these special 'fireproof dwellings'.

Occupying a triangle of land at the north end of the town, where St James' Church still stands, the 'Blocks' contained

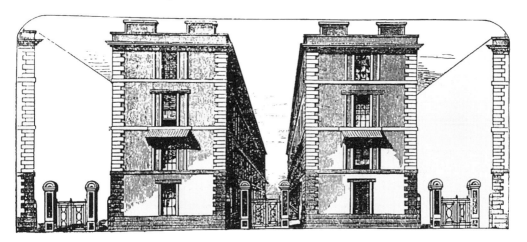

69 *The Dock Cottages—In reality these were tenement blocks of a style often described as 'Scotch flats'.*

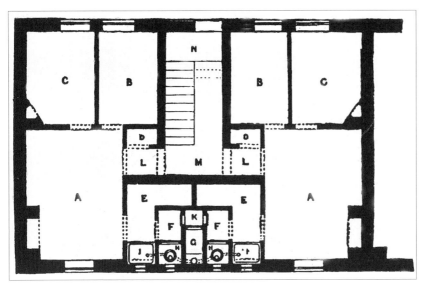

70 *Plan of 'flats' in the Dock Cottages. Though much criticised, these compared well with the housing round Back Chester Street. KEY: A: Living Room, B & C: Bedrooms, D: Cupboard, E: Scullery, F: Water Closet. G: Shaft for soil, gas and water pipes, H: Trapped Pan, I: Sink, the water from which drained into the Trapped Pan, L: Lobby, M: Stairs, N: Entrance.*

324 dwellings, built on four floors. Each unit consisted of a living room and two 'sleeping rooms', an indoor yard or scullery with a sink for washing and a separate water closet. There was a constant supply of water and gas and though the 'cottages' were criticised for their lack of open space, the distance between each block being only six yards, they were infinitely preferable to the alternative noted by the Health Committee, which in September 1846 had reported that there were 'Parties living in huts built of mud in the fields'.

The Dock Cottages had been built at the furthest extremity of the town. Elsewhere a very different kind of development was taking place, that of the residential park or villa estate. The first of these was Parkfield, laid out on a triangle of land bounded by Exmouth Street, Conway Street and Claughton Road, but now only remembered in the names of Park Street, Parkfield and the *Park Hotel*.

The author Hilda Gamlin, who herself lived in Parkfield in a house called Camden Lawn, provides a description:

Parkfield, between Conway Street and Claughton Road, was the first land covered with residences ... In 1835 it was the property of a Mr Dobbs, and his elegant and substantial houses and pleasure grounds, a miniature park, was an incentive for other builders to follow.

Another account comes from Mortimer:

In 1836 a considerable area was purchased in the middle of the township, of which about fifteen acres was laid out as a park ... The inclosure—Parkfield—was soon studded with detached villas, giving a character and appearance to the town that it had not previously enjoyed.

Much better known is nearby Rock Park, laid out by the Liverpool surveyor Jonathon Bennison in 1837. Though cut in half and sadly mutilated by the Rock Ferry Bypass, enough of it survives to give some hint of the place described by the American author Nathaniel

Hawthorne, who lived there from 1853 to 1857 during his time as American Consul in Liverpool.

Clifton Park, across the town boundary in Tranmere, was another villa estate. In 1843 Stansfield, in his sanitary report, described it

> As forming an extremely fine adjunct to the improvements taking place in Birkenhead; a number of elegant mansions are erected, rising one above the other on the hill side as we ascend from the entrance lodge in Grange-road.

Laid out by Walter Scott in the early 1840s, the estate's original appeal was diminished by its proximity to the gas-works and the town's slaughterhouse. Years of neglect, demolition and unimaginative development were allowed to erode its character before it was finally designated a Conservation Area by Wirral Borough Council in the year 2000.

Not all villa building was confined to private parks. In 1842 William Jackson had purchased from Price the greater part of the manor of Claughton as well as the title of lord of the manor. He began to develop his new estate, building for himself Claughton Manor House. Designed by Charles Reed, this was described by Mortimer in great detail:

> The general plan consists of a bold massive centre surrounded by a magnificent Corinthian cornice, and two wings. The principal entrance ... consists of a circular Ionic portico and balustrade. The doorway, which is very elaborate, is surmounted by a carved cornice and trusses, and in the frieze are cornucopiae, vine leaves, and other sculptural decorations, emblematical of hospitality, encircling the armorial bearings of the owner.

71   *Rock Ferry, 1844, C.W.Clennell.*

At the same time the Old Hall was demolished and its grounds, which stretched between Priory Street and Church Street, were developed with new roads, including Leicester Street, White Street and St Mary's Gate.

DEBT AND DISASTER

The 1840s were roller-coaster years for Birkenhead. Almost from the outset the dock scheme ran into trouble. Amendments to the original plans were deemed necessary, involving further legislation and additional expense. In 1845 the Birkenhead Docks Trustees Act authorised the construction of 'docks, walls, warehouses and other works at Birkenhead' (8 & 9 Victoria, c.4, 1845).

The problems were numerous. Setting aside Liverpool's opposition, the scheme was still fraught with difficulties. The contractors were not equal to their task. Costs were underestimated and funds spent rashly. Birkenhead, unlike Liverpool, lacked the banking and insurance houses that might have supported interest in the docks. In addition, the affairs of the town were the subject of bitter feuding, while many of the individuals involved were driven by self-interest and greed.

All this was forgotten for the official opening on 5 April 1847, when fanfares and pageantry masked the essential weakness of the whole enterprise. The following day the *Liverpool Mercury* reported enthusiastically, 'The commercial greatness of Birkenhead has commenced,' but its optimism was unfounded. Within a couple of days William Potter, Chairman of the Dock Committee, received a letter from the General Manager of the North and South Wales Bank which

revealed the true picture. Though the Commissioners had agreed to lower their debt of £58,000, this figure had risen to £64,696. The bank was not prepared to honour any further cheques. In desperation the Commissioners explored other means of raising funds, all to no avail. By August all work on the Docks had ceased. There was simply no more money to complete the work.

The financial difficulties of the Docks was not Birkenhead's only problem. A major source of employment in the town was Lairds' ironworks. On the death of William Laird these passed to his eldest son John. The company was committed to producing iron ships and had built its first iron vessel for the government in the previous year. However, orders were scarce. The Admiralty, an important potential customer but a conservative one, was slow to countenance the use of iron for the Navy, while Lloyds, the marine underwriters, were reluctant to insure iron ships. (They produced a classification for an iron vessel in 1837, but their 'Rules for Iron Ships' did not appear until 1855.) With few orders coming in, work in the shipyards was hard to come by. At the same time the hundreds of temporary migrants who had come to work on the park or Docks departed and there was a dramatic fall in population, with the inevitable reduction in local trade.

DESTITUTION, DISEASE AND DISTRESS

As if these problems were not enough, at a time when the town could least afford to support them, victims of the Irish famine began to arrive. The Vestry minutes recorded the 'great extension of the town, and the great influx from and passing of casual poor to various

Townships and particularly to and from Ireland'. The overseers, responsible for distributing 'out relief,' were overwhelmed by their workload. They were also desperately short of funds, so in January 1847 had taken the unusual step of calling a parishioners' meeting to ask for further subscriptions to the poor rate. The money was forthcoming and 'many thousands of poor people were relieved'.

Most of these 'poor people' had been forced out of Ireland by the failure of the potato harvest. Having sought refuge in Liverpool many then crossed the Mersey to Birkenhead. Mortimer, who witnessed events at first hand, reported:

> Proceeding direct from the ferries to the parish offices, their numbers—principally women and children—were so great, their applications for food so urgent and their destitution so apparent, that the ordinary laws of vagrancy were suspended. In the first quarter of the year no less than upwards of two thousand … applied for assistance.

Inevitably, with times so hard, some individuals turned to crime. One such unfortunate was William McGarry, aged 21, who in January 1847 was sentenced to six months' hard labour at Quarter Sessions for 'stealing at Birkenhead, one half pound weight of Sugar, one ounce weight of Coffee, one quarter of a pound weight of Butter and eight pounds weight of Bread'—a heavy sentence for a small crime. With destitution came 'famine fever', as the Vestry minutes of the time record: 'Typhus Fever does now exist here in a very virulent form among the lower classes of the poor.'

Though a Health Committee had been established, the town had as yet no Medical Officer of Health. Responsibility for the epidemic fell on the Union medical officer, Dr Vaughan, who pressed for a hospital. This, he claimed, 'was absolutely necessary to stay the progress of fever which rages to a great extent and is rapidly increasing among the Poor by the crowded state of the lodging houses'.

The Guardians, ever anxious to save ratepayers' money, reluctantly accepted the need for the temporary fever hospital, housed first in Parkfield then in Livingstone Street.

They also agreed to pay the wages of nurses and two overseer's assistants, deemed necessary 'in consequence of the very great increase in applications for relief'.

The problems persisted. By January 1848 the Guardians' minutes record 'a great increase of Pauperism in Birkenhead'. By March the 'distress' was 'beginning to show itself among the better class of tradesmen'. McGregor Laird, John Laird's younger brother, writing to his wife in the autumn of that year, painted a gloomy picture.

> What do you think of the fallen state of Birkenhead, they have taken the direct Post off and all our letters come and go via Liverpool … Household property and land is literally non-saleable in B'head or L'pool. The ferry boats now run free from 5 to 6 o'clock in the morning and as consequence is an increase of tenants to the small houses about the market.

As if things were not bad enough, the arrival of the Irish famine victims coincided with one of the great pan-

demics of cholera, which reached England in 1848. In Liverpool the outbreak was severe, and in June 1849 Dr Vaughan reported the first victim in Birkenhead. 'A poor Irish woman aged 25, a lodger in one of the crowded lodging houses, No. 64 Field Street—a decided case of asiatic cholera.' Soon other cases appeared, in Back Chester Street and in Tranmere. By the end of the year the death toll from the disease had reached 96.

There was a general downturn in the national economy. In May 1849 the minutes reported the 'present alarming state of the country when the general want of employment is greater than was ever before known'. These were the 'hungry forties' and Birkenhead was not alone.

Not surprisingly, the Commissioners saw their plans for the town founder. Proposals for a cemetery, a college and a hospital had all to be abandoned. Only when the docks on both sides of the water were under one unified, independent body would Birkenhead again flourish.

8

The Town Grows—
Recovery and Representation

CENSUS

> Extensive improvements and building speculation combined with the facilities of steam communication on the Mersey have caused it to become the residence of a portion of the mercantile community of Liverpool.

Thus the 1851 Census explained the growth in Birkenhead's population over the previous decade, a threefold increase from 8,223 to 24,285. Despite the financial difficulties of the Commissioners and the failure of the dock scheme, the town had its attractions. Large villas appeared round the perimeter of the Park and there was more building in the spacious suburb newly laid out by Charles Reed to the south of Devonshire Road and stretching to Manor Hill. In Oxton, too, a series of substantial houses sprang up on the Earl of Shrewsbury's estates. Pre-eminent among the mansions was Jackson's own 'Manor House'. He had been elected MP for Newcastle-under-Lyme in 1846, but retained his old home. With only the inconvenience of a short ferry ride, Liverpool merchants could live in the pleasant surroundings of Claughton and Oxton and still be within easy reach of their work.

CHURCHES, SCHOOLS AND INSTITUTIONS

As the town grew, new churches were built: St John's in Grange Lane, St Anne's in Beckwith Street and St James's, founded to serve the Dock Cottages in the North End. In Claughton, Christchurch, completed in 1849, was consecrated in 1854, and in Oxton, still part of the ecclesiastical parish of Woodchurch, subscriptions were raised to build St Saviour's, consecrated in 1851. The strong Welsh presence was reflected in the opening of a Welsh-speaking church and several chapels.

With the churches came more schools, funded by the denominational societies and offering an elementary education. Attendance was not compulsory and many poorer children, particularly girls, failed to receive even basic schooling:

> St John's Church National Schools, Oliver Street
> Under the management of the Rev. C.J. Hamilton, AB and a Committee.
> Number of Boys 90, Girls 60, Infants 60; Total 240.
> Mr Edward Robinson, master; Miss Redge, mistress; Miss Evans, Mistress of the Infant School.

TO THE INHABITANTS OF BIRKENHEAD,

MATTHEW JONES, Woollen Draper and Tailor, No 12, Chapel Street (opposite the Wesleyan Chapel, Price Street), Birkenhead, in returning thanks to his Friends, and the Inhabitants of Birkenhead and its vicinity, for the liberal support he has received during the last six years he has been in business, begs to say, that nothing shall be wanting on his part to merit a continuance of their favours.

AT Y CYMRU,

MATTHEW JONES a ddymuna ddychwelyd ei ddiolchgarwch i'w Gyfeillion Cymreig, am y gefnogaeth a dderbyniodd. Hefyd y mae yn penderfynu gwasanaethu ei gefnogwyr mor ffyddlon ag y gellir, trwy wneyd gwaith da a hardd am bris rhesymol.

THOMAS H. DRUMMOND, News Agent, Magazine and Periodical Vender, Cigar Divan, Stamp Office, and Public Library, 64, Market street, Birkenhead.

N.B.—Orders Punctually attended to, and forwarded on the day of Publication.
Bookbinding neatly executed on the most reasonable Terms.—Agent to the BIRKENHEAD ADVERTISER.

UPHOLSTERY, CABINET, AND GENERAL FURNISHING ESTABLISHMENT,
(The Oldest existing in the Town,)
GRANGE LANE, BIRKENHEAD.

HENRY SHAW returns his sincere thanks to the Ladies and Gentlemen of the Town and neighbourhood, for the patronage given him, and trusts by supplying,—as heretofore, good articles at moderate prices, to receive a continuance of support.   Ship's Cabins, &c., fitted up.   Every branch of the Upholstery and Cabinet Business carried on as heretofore.   Coffins made on the shortest notice.   Funerals completely and respectably furnished on a moderate scale.

R. STATHAM,
GREEN GROCER, MORPETH DOCK QUAY,
(Near the Shrewsbury Railway Office.)

N.B.—Ships supplied on the Shortest Notice.

73   *Advertisements like this reflected the strong Welsh presence in the town.*

For the better-off there were private establishments, two of them run by the Catholic Sisters, Faithful Companions of Jesus. Their first convent opened in 1849 in Lingdale House, a large mansion in Claughton originally built for William Ravenscroft. Their second, begun in 1852, occupied premises in Hampden Street and Hamilton Square before moving to Holt Hill House in Tranmere. The Lingdale community transferred to Upton Hall in 1863 but Holt Hill continued as a school until 1982. It has since been demolished.

Boys could attend schools in Liverpool, travelling daily across the water. Then in 1860 the Birkenhead Proprietary School opened in Park Road North. It moved to its present site on Shrewsbury Road in 1871, changing its name to Birkenhead School.

For older students there was the Mechanics' Institution and the School of Art and Science, founded in 1855 as part of the Church Institute, Brook Street. The Commissioners' grandiose plans for a Collegiate Institution had foundered but St Aidan's, an independent Theological College, opened in 1846, largely through the efforts of the Rev. Dr Joseph Baylee, the incumbent of Holy Trinity. For 10 years St Aidan's occupied rented premises in Cambridge Terrace, Slatey Road, before moving to a fine Tudor-style building in Howbeck Road. When it closed in the 1960s, the college was demolished and its five acres of ground were covered with houses.

An institution of another sort was the workhouse. The Wirral Union Workhouse at Clatterbridge, erected in 1836-7, was never intended to accommodate the number of paupers who now sought relief in Birkenhead. To deal with their needs the Poor Law Commissioners divided the Wirral Union into two, authorising the construction of a second workhouse in Church Road, Tranmere. This opened in 1863, serving the so-called Commercial Districts of Birkenhead, Wallasey, Tranmere and Bebington. It now forms part of St Catherine's Hospital.

SECTARIANISM AND THE CEMETERY

The 1851 Census recorded some 8,000 Irish people living in Wirral, most of them in Birkenhead. The majority were Catholic and as such were often the focus of religious prejudice. Trouble had

74 *The Manor House, Claughton.*

75 *The last traces of Jackson's Manor House: the former garden gate on Manor Hill.*

76 *St Mary's School. The original school was established by 1829, but money was later raised for the building in Priory Street.*

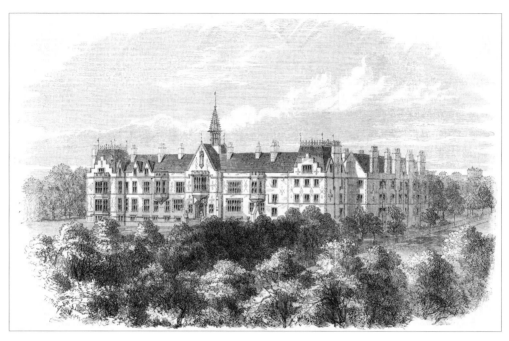

77   *St Aidan's Theological College.—Founded in 1846, it later moved to the building off Forest Road, shown in the illustration. It closed in 1969 and private houses now occupy its site.*

78   *The Wirral Union Workhouse, Church Road, Tranmere, built between 1861 and 1863 to accommodate some 500 inmates. It eventually became St Catherine's Hospital. This photograph shows elderly female residents assembling for an outing organised by the Charles Thompson Mission.*

79 *Plan of Flaybrick Cemetery, laid out by Edward Kemp.*

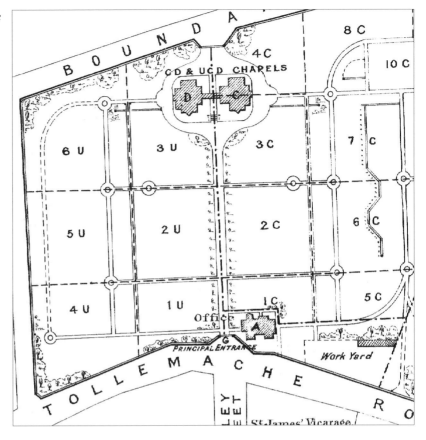

come in 1850 with the announcement that the Pope was to restore the Catholic hierarchy in England. Dr Nicholas Wiseman became Cardinal-Archbishop of Westminster and 12 other bishops were appointed. Across the land there was uproar and in Birkenhead a meeting was organised to protest to the Queen 'on the encroachment of Rome'. As news of the meeting spread, 'a mob of 2,000-3,000 people, chiefly Irish Navigators employed on the Dock works, assembled before the Town Hall.'

The rioters were too many for the Birkenhead police and reinforcements were sent from Liverpool. Their combined attempts to clear the crowd made matters worse. Only with the arrival of Father Browne, priest at St Werburgh's, was calm restored. The meeting was

cancelled and the rioters dispersed. When the meeting reconvened a few days later the offending resolution was passed without incident, Father Browne having persuaded his parishioners to remain at home.

In 1859 plans for a cemetery brought further tension. The town still relied on three burial grounds, none of them satisfactory. At St Mary's, graves had to be excavated from the bedrock, and coffins were placed one on top of another, up to five deep. At St Werburgh's, on the edge of Tranmere Pool, the high water table caused graves to flood, and at the Scotch Church in Conway Street, the schoolroom had been built below the level of the burial ground, with all that that implied. The need for a new cemetery was critical.

BIRKENHEAD ADVERTISER OFFICES, WATERLOO BUILDINGS, BRIDGE STREET.

BOOK-WORK, PAMPHLETS, CATALOGUES, CIRCULARS, CARDS, AND JOBBING IN
GENERAL, DONE WITH NEATNESS AND DESPATCH.

80   Birkenhead Advertiser *masthead.*

Plans for Flaybrick Hill had first been drawn up in the 1840s, before funds ran out. With the scheme resurrected, the town had now to decide whether it should be administered by an independent burial board or by the Commissioners. The Catholics, who were anxious that any cemetery should include a section set aside for their exclusive use, favoured a burial board. John Laird, Chairman of the Commissioners, wanted the cemetery under their control. A poll was held and Laird's proposal won. The Catholics were outraged and turned their venom on the shipyards, gathering there to hurl stones and break windows. In fact their fears were groundless. When Flaybrick opened on 30 May 1864 sections were provided for everyone. So too were separate chapels, one Roman Catholic, one nonconformist and one Anglican. Within ten years some 8,000 burials had taken place.

The most notorious disturbances were the 'Garibaldi Riots' of October 1862. Trouble arose following the announce ment (on orange-coloured posters) of a debate entitled 'Garibaldi and Italy' to be held at the Brook Street Institute, attached to the Protestant Holy Trinity Church. At the time, Garibaldi's attempts to take over the Papal States and his slogan 'Rome or death' made him a hate-figure among the Catholics, and on the night of the meeting large crowds gathered outside Holy Trinity and began attacking its windows. Initially only a small number of police were on hand, but reinforcements arrived led by Superintendent Birnie. Despite his efforts the mob refused to disperse, only doing so when led away by two priests, Fathers Brundit and Gouldon.

On 15 October the abandoned debate took place, provoking further riots:

> 16 October 1862. The Pupil Teachers did not meet for lessons this morning in consequence of the riots last night—opened school at 9.00 am—a very thin attendance compared with yesterday in consequence of the disturbed state of the town. Afternoon dismissed at 3.30 in consequence of the excitement outside. (Logbook, Brunswick Wesleyan School)

A fortnight later trouble flared again and the magistrates sent for soldiers from Manchester. Though these were never deployed, their presence in the town kept things calm. Despite the arrival of several hundred Protestant Orangemen from Liverpool, further clashes were avoided and order was eventually restored.

LIBRARIES, LEISURE AND LEARNED SOCIETIES

On the whole, life in the town flourished. Concerts and lectures took place in the Assembly Rooms and several learned societies were established: the Birkenhead Literary Society in 1848, a Chemical and Philosophical Society, a Medical Society and the Canning and Hamilton Debating Societies. In 1857 came the new Birkenhead Literary and Scientific Society, which at its first meeting heard a paper on 'Geology'.

Until 1855 newspapers were subject to Stamp Duty and so beyond the reach of many readers. To counter this problem various Reading Rooms were established, including the select Birkenhead Subscription News Room in Hamilton Street and the Working Men's Reading Room in Cleveland Street.

> The Birkenhead Working Men's Coffee, Dining & Reading Room, 7 Cleveland Street.
> Coffee 1d. Tea 1½d. Bread 1d. Bread & Butter 2d. Scotch Broth per basin 2½d. Reading Room will be supplied with the most popular Newspapers & Periodicals of the day.
> Terms of Admission 1s. per wk. Single visits 1d. Free to those taking refreshment.
> Open 5.30 am—Ten at night.
> (Advertisement, 1853)

For years Birkenhead lacked its own press, relying on Liverpool for newspapers. Then, in 1853, the *Birkenhead Advertiser* appeared, full of high ideals: 'Our intention is to provide a journal such as the parent may lay upon his table without the fear of any portion of it meeting the eye of his daughters.' It ran for only 28 weeks but was reissued successfully a few years later. A second paper, the *Birkenhead News*, was founded in 1871.

By the 1850s there were several private circulating libraries offering borrowers such works as Mrs Trollope's *The Young Heiress* and Currer Bell's *Villetta*. However, following the Public Libraries Act of 1850 Birkenhead became the first unincorporated borough to have its own public library. On 3 December 1856 a Public Reading Room was opened in Price Street, its hours of 10 a.m. to 1 p.m. and 6 p.m. to 9 p.m. designed to cater for working people. With a stock of 3,132 volumes and some 300 to 400 people visiting daily, it swiftly became a victim of its own success. More space was needed so the library transferred to premises over the new Post Office in Conway Street, opening to the public on 1 May 1857.

Even this accommodation proved inadequate. By 1861 there were 130,000 readers, including 80,000 borrowers described as 'working class', so the Commissioners planned a new library on land they owned in Hamilton Street. This angered a small group of ratepayers who, spurred on by William Jackson, opposed the plans, claiming that building a library would devalue the Commissioners' land. Finally their objections were overcome, and the new library opened on 23 April 1864. To mark the occasion, which coincided with Shakespeare's tercentenary, a specially commissioned marble bust of the playwright was presented to the library by the Literary and Scientific Society. A century and a half later the bust is still on display.

THE STREET RAILWAY

Another 'first' was Birkenhead's tramway, built by the American George Francis Train (1829-1904) in 1860. Train persuaded the Commissioners of the merits of a 'horse railway' which, if constructed, would be the first in the country. Understandably there was opposition from the town's omnibus proprietors but, ignoring this, the Commissioners agreed to Train's scheme. Tram lines were laid and a local coach builder, Robert Main, assembled tram cars from sections imported from America. By August the tramway was complete and a banquet was held to mark its official opening.

Towns everywhere followed Birkenhead's example. To meet the growing demand for tramcars another American, George Starbuck, set up the Starbuck Car & Wagon Co. Ltd, first at Vittoria Wharf and then at 227 Cleveland Street. In 1886 Starbuck sold out to George F. Milnes & Co. Ltd. The two companies between them manufactured some 3,500 tramcars, taking Birkenhead's name all over the world.

81   *Token issued for the street railway.*

THE DOCKS

Though the town was growing, progress in the Docks was slow. Lord Morpeth's words at the official opening, 'The commercial greatness of Birkenhead has begun', now had a hollow ring. After years of planning, all that was complete were 7½ acres of badly constructed dock space. If the scheme was to produce revenue much more was needed.

82   *George Train's street railway car at Birkenhead.*

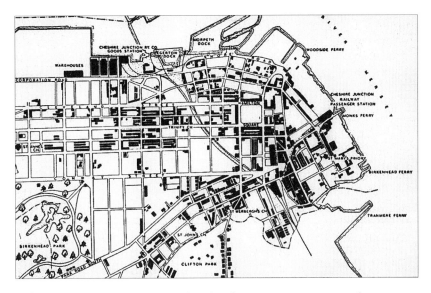

83 *Plan of Birkenhead, 1858, showing the position of Morpeth and Egerton Docks. Many of the streets are still undeveloped.*

In 1849 work resumed. Two temporary dams were constructed, along the lines of the present Duke Street Bridge and Four Bridges, creating a 40-acre basin with access from the river through the Egerton Dock. Named the East Float, this opened in 1851, bringing some increase in local trade. However, costs had far exceeded the funds available and by August 1853 the Dock Trustees were declared 'absolutely insolvent'. Undaunted by this, Thomas Brassey, now a major contractor, offered to complete the scheme, agreeing to be paid in dock bonds. Work began on a further dam across the mouth of the Pool, but in March 1854, when almost complete, this collapsed. Initially Brassey offered to rebuild it at his own expense but when the full costs became apparent he insisted on being paid in cash. With no money available his offer was rejected and once again work on the Docks ceased.

Liverpool now had the opportunity for which it had waited. Virtually bankrupt, the Birkenhead authorities agreed to sell the Docks to their rival, giving Liverpool the monopoly of the whole lower Mersey and the freedom to impose whatever port charges it liked.

Immediately there was an outcry from the cotton importers of Manchester, who campaigned to have the Docks placed in the hands of an independent public body. In 1858 the newly formed Mersey Docks and Harbour Board assumed overall control of both Liverpool and Birkenhead Docks with the authority to complete the Birkenhead dock scheme. This was the turning point for the town. In 1860 the West Float opened, upstream of the Duke Street Bridge. A hydraulic tower was erected to provide power for the dock gates and other machinery and in 1866 the key northern entrances from the river and the new Alfred Dock were officially opened by the Duke of Edinburgh, Queen Victoria's second son.

EMIGRATION

From 1852 to 1865 Birkenhead was the base for a Government Emigrant Depot. Emigration had risen sharply in the 1840s following the Irish famine. Thousands of emigrants converged on Liverpool, staying in filthy, disease-ridden lodging-houses, and were often cheated out of their money by rapacious 'sharpers'. To prevent this the

84   *The opening of the North Docks, 1866.*

authorities decided to establish special depots where the emigrants could be housed and fed in clean surroundings and receive medical checks before embarking. One place considered for the depot was Birkenhead, as McGregor Laird describes:

> 5 October 1848.
> The Emigration Commissioners came down on Monday and spent that day and this at Birkenhead. They talk of compelling all emigrants to land on the Birkenhead Dock Quay, next the river, from the Irish Steamers, there to have a shed where they may be medically examined and then receive a ticket, which will entitle them to a free lodging until they get a ship … The government take up a Block of the Warehouses, fit up the upper floors with Berths as upon a Ship & calculate on always having 2,000–3,000 in them; the vessel is to haul alongside the quay and embark them right off … If they carry this out in the way they talk of it will have an extraordinary effect upon the place.

The first emigrant ship, *The Stranger*, left for Buenos Aires in August 1850, but soon there were regular sailings to Australia. Numbers never reached the levels anticipated by Laird, but servicing the depot brought income to the town:

> The Commissioners now despatch three or four ships a month … The large and well-ventilated dining hall of the depot comfortably accommodates six-hundred people, divided into classes, or schools, of English, Irish and Scottish, each table being so marked. (The *Illustrated London News*, 10 July 1852)

Despite these improvements, passengers often succumbed to disease once on board. In July 1854 cholera broke out on the *Dirigo*, bound for Australia, forcing the ship to turn back and be towed to Birkenhead. The prospect of accommodating both the infected emigrants and the healthy passengers caused consternation among the Commissioners, who urged the authorities to provide 'a hulk' offshore. Their request was refused, so secretly, at dead of night, the passengers were landed and those actually in the throes of cholera taken to a special 'Iron House' swiftly erected for the purpose. Eventually the *Dirigo* re-embarked, sailing on 9 August and reaching Port Adelaide on 22 November, after 15 weeks at sea. The town was happy for the additional trade the depot brought but not keen to shoulder any of the consequences.

CANADA WORKS

In 1852 Thomas Brassey formed the construction firm of Peto, Brassey, Jackson and Betts and won the contract to build the Montréal-to-Toronto section of the Grand Trunk Railway of Canada. All the rolling stock and equipment was to be manufactured in England and shipped out ready-made. Birkenhead was an obvious location for a factory

85   *Brassey Street.*

86   *Emigrant Depot, 1852.*

87   *Cobbles from the boulder road at the Canada Works, relaid at Heap & Partners Ltd, Hoylake.*

and in October 1853 Brassey's Canada Works opened near the head of Wallasey Pool. It was soon employing several hundred men producing locomotives, rails and bridge parts for shipping across the Atlantic.

In 1854 the papers were full of reports from the Crimea, where war had been declared in March. By September the British army found itself in a situation of 'mismanagement' reminiscent of later campaigns. Essential supplies of food, fuel, fodder and clothing were failing to reach the front. The solution was a railway. Confident that he could provide one, Brassey offered to construct a line between the docks at Balaclava and the front at Sebastopol, a distance of 39 miles. A fleet of ships was chartered and supplies and a workforce swiftly assembled. The first group of navvies arrived in Birkenhead on 15 December and were put up in local inns. So efficient was the whole operation that the leading ship, the *Wildfire*, sailed for the Black Sea on 21 December 1854. It was winter, but Brassey's men were well prepared. Packed in their waterproof bags were clothes and kit for any eventuality. The railway was built and Sebastopol finally fell at the end of August 1855, after 349 days of siege.

THE SHIPYARDS

The war brought orders for the shipyards. Laird swiftly set about building two troopships, 16 mortar boats and 14 gunboats. By then the resumption of work on the Docks had forced him to move. In 1852 he leased the Thomas

88   *The Grand Trunk Railway, Canada, is commemorated in the name of this public house.*

Vernon yard in Liverpool and in 1853 shifted his Birkenhead operations to the head of Wallasey Pool. There he might have stayed had his request to make breaks in the Dock Wall not been turned down. An alternative site was located directly on the Mersey.

> In consequence of arrangements connected with the completion of the Birkenhead Docks ... Mr Laird has taken a new yard fronting the river at Birkenhead, where he has constructed from the designs of Mr James Abernethy, C.E. of London, four graving docks, and a gridiron, and extensive workshops of various kinds, requisite for the ... building and repairing ships of iron and wood, and the making of boilers and repairing machinery. These works have been executed in about two years and are expected to be in full operation by the end of the year. (The *Illustrated London News*, 25 October 1856)

By 1857 the move was complete and the Liverpool yard given up. The first ship built in Church Street, the *Pintando*, was launched in November and three weeks later came celebrations.

> Last night [wrote Macgregor Laird] John gave a dinner to his foreman and Tradespeople, about 50—at the *Monks Ferry Hotel*—presented to Richard a Silver Teakettle, very handsome, with an inscription. He has been 30 years and upwards with him and his father and to McNicol, who had been 20 years in the office and lately set up for himself, a Silver Teapot. All went off very well—the men a very reputable lot, some very fine heads among them—lots of singing, toasts and speeches.

It was through Macgregor that the new yard secured the contract for the *Ma Robert*, a small river steamer ordered by the government for David Livingstone and named after his wife. The vessel was made of steel plates and constructed in three sections for lightness and ease of transport to Africa. Sadly, Livingstone's misuse of her meant she was not a success. Macgregor had had a long association with Africa, voyaging to West Africa in the early 1830s and venturing up the Niger, hoping that by promoting legitimate trade he could help bring an end to slavery. Subsequently he acted as secretary to the Birkenhead Dock Company and helped found the African Steamship Navigation Company, a forerunner of the Elder Dempster Line.

Macgregor Laird died in January 1861, never to know of the one event which marred his brother's career. In 1861 the outbreak of the American Civil War brought divided loyalties. The Queen proclaimed Britain's neutrality but on Merseyside many businessmen sympathised with the Confederate cause. Control of Laird's yards had passed to his sons so it was they who, in July 1861, accepted the order to build vessel 'No. 290' for the American James Bulloch, apparently acting privately but in reality an agent of the Confederate Navy. The vessel, launched in 1862 as the *Enrica*, became the commerce raider CSS *Alabama*. For two years she attacked Union ships before being sunk in 1864. As compensation for her actions the British government were forced to pay the United States £3 million.

PARLIAMENTARY REPRESENTATION
Vessel 'No. 290' was still on the stocks when in December 1861 Laird became

89   *Laird's Yard, 1861.*

90   *The Alabama.*

91 *Iron-clad steam ram, intended for the Confederate navy. It was seized in October 1863 and later renamed HMS* Scorpion.

92 *The explosion of the* Lottie Sleigh, *1864. The ship, loaded with gunpowder, caught fire and exploded when a paraffin lamp was upset in the hold. No one was killed but property in Birkenhead suffered considerable damage.*

93   *Portrait of John Laird, 1861.*

Conservative. Against him the Liberals put up Thomas Brassey, the 25-year-old son of the contractor. On Election Day polling booths were erected in Birkenhead, Bebington, Claughton, Oxton and Tranmere and, anticipating trouble, the police gathered in force. As it was, the day passed without incident and 2,999 of the town's 3,489 registered electors turned out to vote. 'Three cheers for Laird. Hurrah! Hurrah! Hurrah!' wrote the irrepressible George Francis Train, congratulating Laird on his victory. Three times more Laird was returned, serving Birkenhead as MP until his death in 1874.

BENEFACTIONS

As a gesture of thanks for his election, Laird founded the town's first purpose-built hospital. For years there had been a dispensary and later a hospital, both funded by voluntary contributions and housed in rented premises. The numbers treated increased every year. In 1859 there were 4,064 patients, 153 in the hospital and 3,911 at the dispensary. Larger premises were essential and a site for these was found facing the Park. Thomas Brassey contributed

the town's first MP. 'Birkenhead will be up and stirring,' said the *Manchester Guardian*, at the news that the town had been awarded a seat, and certainly there was much stirring as the Register of Electors was compiled. Laird stood as a

BIRKENHEAD HOSPITAL AND DISPENSARY.
WANTED, for the Birkenhead Hospital and Dispensary, (in consequence of the Death of Mr. W. R. CROUCH,) a HOUSE SURGEON and APOTHECARY, who must devote his services exclusively to the Institution, at a Salary of £80 per Annum, with Board and Lodging. No Person is eligible who is not a Member of the College of Surgeons of London, Dublin, or Edinburgh, or of the Faculty of the Physicians and Surgeons at Glasgow, and who is not competent to prepare the Medicines prescribed by the Honorary Medical Officers. Testimonials of Character and Qualification to be sent to the Secretary, Mr. W. W. ST. GEORGE, Holt-hill, Birkenhead, on or before the 24th November instant.   The Candidates will be examined personally and by their Testimonials, at the Hospital, on TUESDAY, the 28th November instant, at Six o'Clock, p.m., and the Election will take place on the following Morning.   Unmarried Parties only need apply.
   Birkenhead, November 2d, 1854.

94   *Advertisement for a House Surgeon and Apothecary placed in the* Lancet.

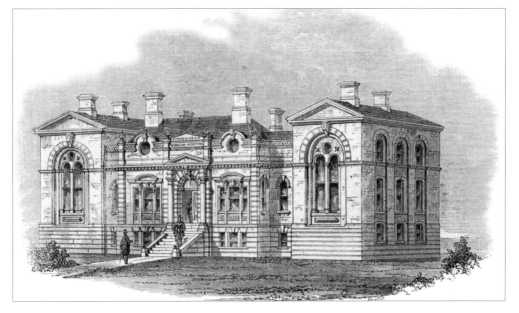

95   *The Hospital.*

£500 towards its cost, and a local architect, Walter Scott, drew up plans. In November 1862 the foundation stone was laid and the hospital opened in 1863. The next year the town appointed its first Medical Officer of Health.

Not to be outdone in generosity, William Jackson provided a building for the newly founded Albert (Memorial) Industrial School, a 'ragged school'

intended for the poorest children in the town. This opened in Corporation Road in 1865, the exhortation over its main entrance reading, 'Train up a child in the way he should go, and when he is old he will not depart from it.'

In 1871 Laird made a further gift to the town of a new School of Art, a home for the art school already established in connection with the Free Library. Two

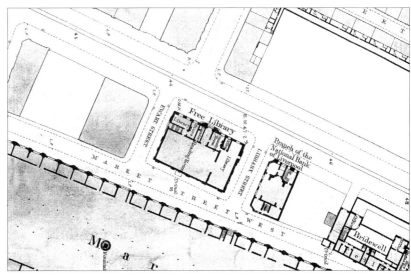

96   *Map showing the new public library, Hamilton Street, opened in 1864.*

97 *Albert Memorial Industrial School, completed in 1865. Prince Albert had died of typhoid in 1861 and memorials were erected in his name.*

years later, in 1873, he died. On the day of his funeral, work stopped in the town and hundreds followed his coffin to St Mary's cemetery. Subsequently a memorial statue was erected in his honour, originally placed in the centre of Hamilton Square.

The same decade saw the death of his two contemporaries, Thomas Brassey and William Jackson. All three had been born in 1806, all three had served as Improvement Commissioners and all three had been closely involved with the development of the town. Brassey died first, in 1870, and Jackson, by then Sir William Jackson, in 1876. It was the end of an era. Within a year of Jackson's death Birkenhead became a Borough and the old Improvement Commissioners met for the last time in November 1879.

98 *Birkenhead School of Art, opened in 1871.*

9

The Borough
Late Victorian and Edwardian
Birkenhead

INCORPORATION

In 1875 five men, Joseph Craven, Charles Willmer, William Worrall, William Fulton and Edward Bevan, began a campaign to have Birkenhead made a Borough. Since 1838 the town's affairs had been in the hands of just 21 Improvement Commissioners, elected by only the wealthiest of its residents. Borough status would allow Birkenhead to elect a larger council and would extend the vote to many more ratepayers, thus making the town fathers more accountable to their electorate.

An element of the scheme was to bring Birkenhead, with a population of 52,581, Claughton (2,937), Oxton (3,500), Tranmere (18,517) and the Rock Ferry portion of Bebington (3,000) under one single authority. This made sense as the built-up area had spread far beyond the town's original boundaries, engulfing the neighbouring townships. Nevertheless, there was fierce opposition to the scheme, particularly in Tranmere, where residents wanted to retain their separate identity, fearing an increase in the rates. Petitions and counter-petitions

winged their way to Westminster and only after a Public Inquiry did the Privy Council reach its decision:

> We therefore do hereby grant and declare that the inhabitants of the said town of Birkenhead, embracing the whole of the township of Birkenhead and the several districts of Claughton, otherwise Claughton-cum-Grange, Oxton, Tranmere and part of the township and district of Higher Bebington, and their successors, shall be for ever hereafter one body politic and corporate in deed, fact and name, and that the said body corporate shall be called 'The Mayor, Aldermen, and Burgesses of the Borough of Birkenhead'.

The Charter of Incorporation was issued on 13 August 1877 and on 14 November Birkenhead duly elected a mayor, aldermen and a full town council: 40 Conservatives and two Liberals. Appropriately the first mayor was John Laird junior, third son of John Laird, grandson of William Laird. Ambrose

Assessment for local rates, 1876				
	Birkenhead	Claughton	Oxton	Tranmere
Population	52,481	2,937	3,500	18,517
Dwelling houses	8,100	340	500	3,446
Local rates	3s.2d	3s.2d	1s. 10d.	2s. 3d

95

Waln remained as Clerk and William Hardisty as Treasurer, and the old and new committees were organised on almost identical lines.

THE NEW TOWN HALL

With the Council established it was decided to build a new Town Hall. A larger and more imposing building would add prestige to the fledgling Borough and a site had been earmarked for just this purpose on Gillespie Graham's original plan. In October 1881 *The Builder* announced a competition for a suitable design, costing no more than £43,000. The judge was Charles Barry junior, son of Sir Charles Barry, architect of the Houses of Parliament, and a respected architect in his own right. Of the 138 entrants, the winner was a Liverpool man, Charles Ellison. His proposal, reminiscent of Bolton Town Hall, was for a classical building, very much 'in keeping' with the rest of Hamilton Square, to be built of a combination of Scottish granite and Storeton stone. It would have a pillared portico and a 200ft domed clock tower.

Almost immediately there was disagreement, *The Builder* maintaining that the proper place for Ellison's design was in the centre of Hamilton Square. Fortunately this suggestion was ignored and on 10 October 1883 Thomas Deakin, the mayor, laid the foundation stone on the site originally selected. Three years later, on 29 November 1886, the tower clock was set in motion by Elsie Laird, the daughter of William Laird, mayor for that year. To mark the occasion Elsie was given a little ivory sewing case. Finally, on 10 February 1887, the wedding anniversary of Queen Victoria and Prince Albert, came the official opening. Costs had spiralled to £52,000, well in excess of the original budget, but this was forgotten in the celebrations of the day.

The next year, under the terms of the 1888 Local Government Act, Birkenhead, with a population reaching 99,000, became a County Borough. Hitherto part of Cheshire, it was now completely self-governing, though many of its townsfolk still felt themselves Cestrians at heart.

99 *The east side of Hamilton Square, before the building of the new Town Hall. The ghost-like figures, on the near side of the square, are people moving in front of the camera.*

100 *Design for the new Town Hall, officially opened in 1887.*

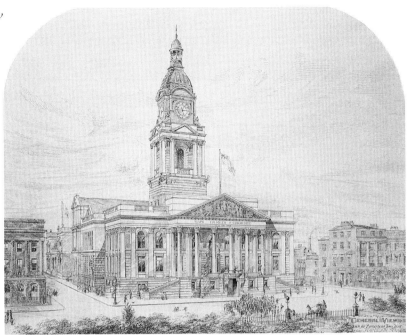

A Charter of Quarter Sessions had been awarded to Birkenhead in 1882, so while the Town Hall went up in Hamilton Square a new Sessions House rose behind it in Chester Street. The architects were T.D. Barry & Sons and the new building, also classical in style and constructed of Storeton stone, was opened in 1887.

Soon more work became necessary. Electric light had been installed in the Town Hall and on 10 July 1901, following a meeting of the Water Committee, the lights in the Council Chamber fused. This started a fire which so badly damaged the clock tower it had to be completely remodelled and caused such extensive devastation that for a whole year council meetings were held in the Sessions House while the building was repaired.

EDUCATION AND THE SCHOOL BOARD

One duty for which the Corporation was not responsible was the provision of schools. The 1870 Education Act authorised the establishment of School Boards to provide public elementary schools wherever there was a shortfall in places. Inevitably in Birkenhead, the very notion of a Board with powers to levy a rate met with opposition. The general feeling was that it would be better (and cheaper) to leave the provision of schools in the hands of the voluntary societies.

In 1880 school attendance became compulsory for all children aged five to ten and in Birkenhead there were insufficient places for the school age population. Undaunted, the authorities airily dismissed these uncomfortable statistics with the claim that they included an 'above average' proportion of the 'upper classes', all likely to be educated privately. In place of a Board, a School Extension Committee was formed to expand school accommodation through voluntary donations rather than the rates.

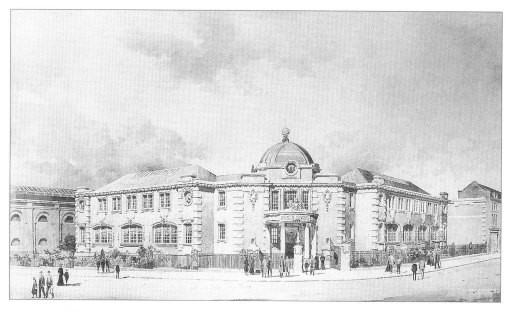

101   *Architect's drawing of the Carnegie Library, Market Street, opened in 1909.*

Unfortunately the numbers of children continued to grow, and in 1893 the Borough's hand was forced.

> The lords of the Committee on Education order that a resolution be sent to the Mayor of Birkenhead requiring him to take proceedings for the holding of elections for a School Board for the whole Borough within 28 clear days.

Elections duly took place on 10 May, two days short of the deadline. Over half of the 15,000 strong electorate voted, returning 15 of the 37 candidates. Once elected, the new Board set about 'plugging the gaps', building The Woodlands, Cathcart Street and Well Lane Schools and providing a permanent building for Laird Street School.

But the Board, so long resisted, had only a short life. In 1903, following the 1902 Education Act, it was superseded by the Education Committee. The Council was now responsible for school

provision right across the age range and in consequence embarked on a major school building programme including new schools in Conway Street (1903), Hemingford Street (1909) and Brassey Street (1911). The number of pupils in the voluntary schools declined while those in the Council's schools doubled from 4,619 in 1903 to 9,812 in 1914.

Private initiative also played its part. In 1882 the Borough's first girls' secondary school opened, the Higher Tranmere High School for Girls. In 1885 came Birkenhead High School, occupying the former Oxton Local Board Offices in Village Road. In 1889 Birkenhead Institute opened in Whetstone Lane. Its most famous pupil, a small, dark-haired boy, Wilfred Owen, entered the preparatory department in 1900, aged seven. He stayed until 1907, when his family moved to Shrewsbury. A year later the Education Committee took over the Institute, the two High Schools remaining independent.

Corporation Depot, Cleveland Street (1904) and the General Post Office, Argyle Street (1908). In addition, with funds from the Carnegie Foundation, both the North Branch Library (1908) and the South Branch Library (1909) were rebuilt and a new Central Library opened in Market Square.

On a more mundane note, a pioneering improvement scheme followed the Housing of the Working Classes Act of 1890. A network of unsanitary courts, just south of the Market, was swept away and Tunnel Road, Egerton Street and Getley Street took their place. More dwellings were put up in Green Lane and Mason Street off the New Chester Road and by 1914 the total number of new homes erected by the Corporation numbered 3,081 houses and 316 flats.

In 1890 Birkenhead became one of the first authorities to produce its own electricity supply. A 'Generating Station' was built in Bentink Street and in September 1896 the service began. In the same year the Corporation sought permission to electrify the trams, which

HOUSING AND PUBLIC BUILDINGS

Schools were not the only new buildings to appear. In 1883 the Children's Hospital, founded in 1869, moved into purpose-built premises in Woodchurch Road. At the same time the old 'Lying in Hospital', originally in Clifton Crescent, took over a large private house in Grange Mount which was used as a maternity hospital. In 1895 the new Hospital for Infectious Diseases opened in Tollemache Road, on the slopes of Bidston Hill, replacing the old Fever Hospital in Livingstone Street.

Other public buildings included the Fire Station in Whetstone Lane (1895), the abattoir on the New Chester Road (1896), the impressive Poor Law Offices in Conway Street (1899), the Tram Terminus, Laird Street (1903), the

103 *Interior of the children's room, Birkenhead Library.*

104 *Market traders, 1919.*

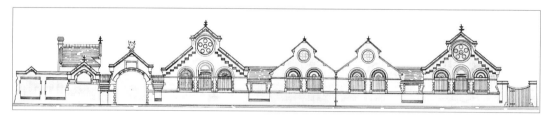

105 *Design for the abattoir.*

CORPORATION ELECTRICITY DEPARTMENT

LIST OF CHARGES

SIMPLE HIRE

Cooking Stoves – From **6/-** per Quarter, for first 18 months, and **3/-** per Quarter thereafter.

Cookerettes – From **3/6** per Quarter, for first 18 months, and **2/-** per Quarter thereafter.

	per Quarter
Breakfast Cookers	from **2/-**
Grilles	...**1/3**
Fires	...**1/6**
Irons	...**1/3**
Kettles	...**2/-**
Urns	...**2/6**
Wash Boilers	...**4/6**

106 *Table of Electricity Charges.*

it acquired in 1899. A second generating station was built in Craven Street and in 1910 the two operations merged. Further expansion was impossible, so to meet the demands of its customers the Corporation bought in extra supplies from Wallasey and, after the road tunnel opened, even from Liverpool.

Many of these buildings, including the generating stations, were built in bright red Ruabon brick with elaborate terracotta detailing and, often, the Borough's coat of arms. One architect who favoured this brick and worked extensively in the Borough was Edmund Kirby (1838-1920). Originally an assistant to the great Chester architect, John Douglas, he established his own practice in Liverpool in 1867, making Birkenhead his home. From 1897 he lived at Overdale, Beresford Road, where, a devout Catholic, he built the little Church of the Holy Name in his own orchard. His other churches included St Laurence, Price Street, which replaced a church made unsafe by the railway tunnel, and St Joseph's, North Road, Tranmere. Among his secular buildings were Redcourt, Devonshire Place, built for the banker George Rae, and Mere Hall in Noctorum.

Recreation and Sport

With electricity now available, a new form of entertainment became popular. In November 1896 the Argyle Music Hall became the first theatre outside London to show Eddison's Vitagraph 'living pictures', a special cable being run to the theatre for the occasion. Soon the Queen's Hall and the Theatre Royal began showing 'animated pictures' and in 1913 the Claughton Music Hall re-opened as the Claughton Picture Palace.

Indoor recreation was provided by the Baths. The Argyle Street South Baths opened in 1882, offering not just washing facilities (very important when so many homes lacked bathrooms) but also a swimming pool. In 1900 two more pools became available when the North End Baths opened in Livingstone Street.

For outdoor activities there were the parks, the original Birkenhead Park and Mersey Park, Tranmere, opening in 1885, Victoria Park, Tranmere, opening in 1901 and the Arno, Oxton, opening in 1912. For those prepared to venture further afield, the Corporation was also responsible for Thurstaston Common, Bidston Hill and Great Meols Common.

There was also provision for organised sport. Birkenhead Cricket Club had played in the Park from 1846 and the Rugby Club from 1871.

107 *Poster for the Argyle Theatre, Birkenhead, built for Dennis Grannel and opened as a Music Hall in 1868. In 1876 it became known as The Prince Of Wales Theatre but reverted to its original name in 1890.*

108   *Birkenhead Cricket Club, founded in 1846.*

Association football followed. Among the early clubs were Birkenhead Football Club, Birkenhead Argyle, Birkenhead Rovers and Belmont, the latter formed to provide a winter alternative to cricket for members of Lyndhurst Wanderers and the Belmont Cricket Club, both offshoots of the Wesleyan Chapel Sunday School, Whitfield Street.

Belmont's 'first season' was reported in the *Birkenhead News* of 1884 and in September 1885 came the decision to change its name to 'Tranmere Rovers'. The history of the resulting club is well known. It played first on 'Steele's Field' in what was then Prenton Lane, and then in 1887 at Ravenshaw's Field, off Temple Road, a pitch later renamed Prenton Park. By 1912 it had moved to its present site at the bottom of Prenton Road West.

WOODSIDE STATION AND THE MERSEY RAILWAY TUNNEL

The later 19th century and the early 20th century brought considerable changes

in transport. In March 1878 the Joint London & North Western and Great Western Railway opened a new main line station on the south side of Woodside, driving a tunnel under Church Street and closing their old terminus at Monks' Ferry to all but coaling trains.

At the same time work was proceeding on the Mersey rail tunnel. The ferry was still the sole means of crossing the river and, though the installation of a floating landing stage in 1861 and the use of larger vessels had improved the service, cross-river travellers still faced being tossed about whenever the weather was rough.

The scheme for the tunnel, first proposed in 1866, was approved in 1871 and work finally began in 1879. The contractor was Major Samuel Isaac and the sub-contractors Waddells of Edinburgh, with James Brunlees and Charles Douglas Fox acting as Engineers in Chief. When their pilot heading proved successful, tunnelling began on both sides of the river. In

109 *The interior of Woodside Station, opened in 1878, looking up towards the* Woodside Hotel.

1881 William Laird set in motion a giant steam engine designed to pump water from the tunnel. In 1883 a Beaumont rock-boring machine was introduced, increasing the pace of work. Finally, on 17 January 1884, came the breakthrough, marked by a ceremony attended by the mayors of both towns. By December 1885 the tunnel was complete and the public were invited to walk through.

Initially the line ran only between Green Lane in Tranmere and James Street in Liverpool, with intermediate stations at Birkenhead Central and Hamilton Square, where an ornate brick tower housed a hydraulic lift to bring passengers to the surface. In 1888 a branch line opened to Birkenhead Park and in 1891 the Green Lane line was extended to Rock Ferry. Finally, in 1895, a direct link was laid to the Birkenhead-Chester line.

The official opening was performed by the Prince of Wales, later Edward VII, who, with his two sons, travelled through the tunnel from Green Lane

110 *The hydraulic tower at the Mersey Rail Station, Hamilton Square.*

to Liverpool on 20 January 1886. The regular service began in February and at first seemed likely to eclipse the ferry in popularity but, as passengers found themselves engulfed in smoke and steam, numbers dwindled. As with so many of Birkenhead's ventures, bankruptcy loomed and in two years the company was in the hands of the receiver.

The solution was electrification, already in use for the Borough's trams. In 1900 permission was given to electrify the railway, new tracks were laid and new rolling stock acquired. With remarkable efficiency, the last steam train left Liverpool at midnight on 2 May 1903 and electric operations began the next day. The line was thus the first in the country to run entirely on electricity. With a service not only speedy but clean, the company at last began to make a profit. Only Birkenhead's market traders and shopkeepers were unhappy, fearing a loss in trade.

CHANGES ON THE WATERFRONT

By 1880 the main dock system was complete. On the north side of the East Float were grain warehouses and mills and on the newly opened Wallasey Dock and at Woodside were the 'Foreign Animal Wharves' or Lairages, used to house and slaughter imported cattle. In 1885 the Vacuum Oil Company established itself at the far end of the West Float, near the Penny Bridge, and at several points there were coal drops for the all-important task of coaling ships.

For those employed on the Docks work was hard and dangerous. In 1881 Francis Vacher, the Medical Officer of Health, reported on 'the many sudden deaths' occurring there. The worst accident came in 1909. Lack of adequate berthing space and the increasing size of ships had led the Dock Board to build a new dock at Vittoria Wharf, an area of reclaimed land on the East Float. It was during work on it that a coffer dam collapsed, killing 14 men and injuring three. Only seven of the workforce escaped.

The increasing size of ships was a problem for Lairds, who were losing orders for liners and large cargo steamers as their yard was too small. Room for

111 *Label for a goods truck on the Seacombe, Hoylake & Deeside Railway. The line later became part of the Wirral railway and the Dock Station was renamed Birkenhead North.*

112 *The Cheshire Lines building, Canning Street, a former railway warehouse.*

expansion was restricted but in 1900 the company acquired land to the south and the yard was enlarged. To make way for the new docks, the Royal Mersey Yacht Club, which rented the old Birkenhead ferry slipway, moved to Rock Ferry and the private houses on Mersey Street disappeared.

In 1903 Lairds underwent a merger with the Sheffield steel firm Charles Cammell, becoming Cammell Laird and Co. Ltd under the chairmanship of the fourth generation of Lairds, J. MacGregor Laird. The cost of expansion was high and until 1909 the new company ran at a loss, taking on fewer men.

PHILANTHROPY

Within the Borough there were great inequalities of wealth and for anyone out of work life was hard. In November 1904 the Electricity Committee noted the 'slackness of trade' and the Mayor received a deputation concerned about 'the exceptional distress in the town'. A Relief Fund was opened and subscriptions invited.

An offer by the Choral Society to give 'a rendition of Handel's *Messiah*' was refused but contributions from the Hot Pot Fund of 200 cwt of coal, and from the Maypole Dairy Company of 500 cards for '¼lb of best margarine' were accepted. Payments were made towards meals for schoolchildren and for 'clogs and stockings'. (A request for a false leg was passed on to the Charity Organisation Society.)

Among the poorest families the plight of children was dire. One man who set out to improve things was Charles Thompson (1841-1903). A devout nonconformist, he had come to Birkenhead for its 'balmy ozone and health-giving breeze'. Managing a grocer's shop in Price Street during the day, he organised meetings for local children in his spare time. Soon the 'Mission' took over his life and after various moves he established it in its present home, the former Friends' Meeting House in Hemingford Street, purchased for him by a group of supporters and officially opened on 9 January 1892.

113   *Barefoot but happy. Little boys pose outside the Charles Thompson Mission, Hemingford Street.*

Thompson died in 1903 but his daughter Annie continued his work. Always aware of the value of publicity the Mission took numerous photographs: children, barefoot with heads shaved against lice, the blind and elderly receiving cups of tea, 'The Crowning of the May Queen', 'Children on Empire Day', 'Loyal little hearts under threadbare jackets', river trips, summer outings, sales of work and numerous Christmas parties.

Another person concerned for young people was William Norris (1862-1934), who in 1886 founded the Shaftesbury Boys' Club for 'street boys and working lads'. The club was popular and as membership grew it moved from rooms in Chester Street to a former chapel in Jackson Street, opening additional premises in Thomas Street in 1911.

The YMCA and the YWCA were also represented in the town, providing hostels and recreational facilities. In 1890 the YMCA moved from Conway Street

114   *Little girls on the steps of the Mission. The building was originally the Friends' Meeting House.*

to new headquarters in Grange Road. There, on 22 November 1906, General Sir Robert Baden-Powell, the hero of Mafeking, gave a talk on 'Peace Scouts'. Over the next months he gave more talks, visiting various YMCAs before returning to Birkenhead on 24 January 1908 to 'publicly inaugurate' the Scout Movement. Following his visit, local boys formed perhaps the first troops ever, the 1st and 2nd Birkenhead Scouts.

In April 1910 Baden-Powell came again, this time to unveil a plaque commemorating the inauguration. Sadly, the Grange Road building where this ceremony took place became a shop when the YMCA moved to Whetstone Lane in 1937. The Scouts remembered the role played by Birkenhead in their formation and in 1929, when they 'came of age', held their World Jamboree in Arrowe Park.

115   *The YMCA in Grange Road.*

THE VOTE

In 1906 Birkenhead elected its first Labour councillor, the boilermaker Sam Vaughan, who represented Cleveland Ward. It also broke its long links with the Conservatives and elected Henry Harvey Vivian as a Lib-Lab MP. In the same year the famous 'F.E.' Smith, born in Pilgrim Street in 1872, was returned as MP for Walton in Liverpool. He would later become Lord Chancellor, taking the title Lord Birkenhead.

Until 1918 only men could vote. In Birkenhead a branch of the Women's Suffrage Society was formed and by the new century it was campaigning vociferously. Women from several of Birkenhead's influential families joined the cause, holding open-air meetings at the Park gates, chalking slogans on pavements and even journeying to London to join major demonstrations.

116   *Plaque commemorating the inauguration of Scouting.*

117   *6, James Street, home of the Ker family and the hiding place for the 'Lady Dodgers' on Census night, 1911.*

as they were called by the *Birkenhead News*, claimed that since the aim of the census was to gather information on 'citizens', women, who did not have 'citizens' rights', should not take part. On census night over fifty protesters gathered at the Kers' house and evaded the count.

In 1912 Dr Ker hit the headlines again when she was sent to Holloway for smashing windows at Harrods. Not surprisingly, the respectable committees on which she served asked her to resign. Margaret, meanwhile, was arrested for setting fire to a pillar box and sentenced to three months in prison. As a medical student at Liverpool University she should have faced expulsion but, supported by the Vice Chancellor, her only penalty was to loose the £30 bursary awarded her by the Birkenhead Education Committee.

The most prominent suffragette was Dr Alice J. Stewart Ker (1853–1943). Born in Banffshire, she trained as a doctor and became only the 13th woman to have her name added to the Medical Register. In 1888 she had settled in Birkenhead with her husband Edward, a Liverpool merchant, and was duly appointed Honorary Medical Officer to the Children's Hospital, the Lying-In Hospital and the Birkenhead Rescue Home.

In 1909 the now widowed Dr Ker and her eldest daughter, Margaret, joined the militant Women's Social and Political Union. In 1911 their house, 6 James Street, was the base for a 'Census Strike'. The 'strikers', or 'Lady Dodgers'

THE DELLA ROBBIA POTTERY: 1894–1906

In the art world Birkenhead is renowned for its Della Robbia Pottery, named after the Florentine sculptor Luca della Robbia and established at 2A Price Street in 1894. Its founder was Harold Rathbone (1858–1929), a member of the well-to-do Liverpool family and a painter, designer and poet. He and his partner, the sculptor Conrad Dressler (1856–1940), were both inspired by the ideas of William Morris and the Pre-Raphaelites.

At first the Pottery used local clay dug from pits at Moreton. When this proved coarse and difficult to fire, supplies from elsewhere were

118 *Former Della Robbia Pottery, Price Street.*

119 *Della Robbia—Group of potters.*

120   *Della Robbia—The Mason Vase.*

collection and more are displayed in the Wirral Museum. Particularly striking is the 'Mason Vase' made to commemorate a visit to the Pottery by Princess Louise on 21 January 1898. The vase was designed by Miss Cassandia Annie Walker, the most talented of the Della Robbia decorators, and bears the arms of the Corporation. It was presented to Mr Edward Mason, the mayor of the day.

LEE'S TAPESTRY WORKS

Birkenhead was also home to another enterprise influenced by the ideals of William Morris. This was A.H. Lee and Sons' Tapestry Works, which from 1908 to 1970 operated in Stanley Road. Known affectionately as 'The Tap', it offered employment to generations of Birkenhead women as well as to men.

Arthur Lee (1853-1932) had begun the business in Bolton before moving first to Warrington and then to Birkenhead. In an era of increased mass-production, he was keen to see handwork play a part in textile manufacture. His Jacquard looms were mechanised but his workers also undertook crewel embroidery, hand needlework and the hand blocking of designs. The fabrics thus produced were of exceptional quality. One customer, Cunard, used them to furnish the state rooms of its liners. Another special commission was for the tapestry depicting Edward III granting a charter to the monks of Birkenhead in 1330. This particular piece contained over ¼ million stitches.

Lee's idealism was not confined to textiles. Hundreds of the Borough's children benefited from holidays spent at the camps he founded at Dyserth and

substituted. Dressler, an idealistic advocate of the use of local labour and local materials, felt his principles compromised and in 1897 he left for the south. His place was taken by another sculptor, Carlo Manzoni (1855-1910), who remained with Rathbone until the Pottery closed.

The output of the Pottery included tiles, earthenware and relief plaques, and their designs incorporated the floral and figural motifs characteristic of the Art Nouveau and Arts and Crafts traditions. Entirely hand-made, pieces were expensive to produce, and though the Pottery's customers included Liberty & Co. of London it was never a financial success and was forced into voluntary liquidation in 1906.

Today examples of Della Robbia Ware are much sought after. The Williamson Art Gallery holds a large

121   *The Tapestry Works. In the left foreground are some of the Dock cottages.*

122   *A tapestry, showing the granting of the 'charter of ferryage' to Birkenhead Priory by Edward III in 1330; one of the many fine pieces made at A.H. Lee & Sons' Tapestry Works.*

123 *Eleanor Cross, Hamilton Square, erected in honour of the life of Queen Victoria and unveiled in 1905.*

Ruthin, and his Wednesday night Magic Lantern Shows were legendary among the families of the North End.

ROYAL EVENTS

In Birkenhead royal events were always the occasion of ceremony. In 1897 the Queen's Diamond Jubilee was celebrated with exuberance, notwithstanding the torrential rain. On the river there was a marine display and in the evening fireworks. Four years later, in 1901, the town mourned Victoria's death. A subscription list was opened and Edmund Kirby was commissioned to design an appropriate monument to commemorate her reign. John Laird's statue was moved from the centre of Hamilton Square and in 1905 a replica Eleanor Cross took its place.

Victoria was succeeded by her eldest son, Edward VII, and to mark his reign a 'Coronation Oak' was planted in the Park. In 1910 he, too, was dead, and the Edward VII Memorial Clock Tower (1912), designed by Edmund Kirby & Sons, was raised in his memory in Argyle Street.

In the long hot summer of 1911 came the coronation of George V. There were murmurings of labour unrest, but at Woodside 'Long live our King, G.R.' was picked out in lights and there were bonfires and fireworks in the parks. No one could foresee that within three years the King would visit a town busily preparing for war.

124 *Edward VII Memorial Clock Tower, in its original location in Argyle Street before it was moved to Clifton Crescent. The Argyle Theatre is visible in the background.*

10

Birkenhead in Peace and War

THE FIRST WORLD WAR

Birkenhead, as a major ship-building and repair centre and a reception port for trans-Atlantic convoys, played a key role in both world wars. However, at the start of 1914 the event uppermost in the Council's mind was the impending visit of King George V and Queen Mary. The royal couple were to tour Cammell Lairds and then the King was to open officially the most recently acquired section of Bidston Hill before going on to open Wallasey Town Hall. The papers published details of the royal route, and local shops advertised supplies of flags and bunting:

> Flags, Codes and Decorations for sale at Jones' Albert House, Price Street.

Stands for spectators went up outside the Town Hall and the tram stops were repainted. Children were given time off school and each child received a souvenir: Frank Fox's *The British Empire*, with 'Coloured Illustrations and the Arms of the Borough on the Front', for the seniors, medals for the juniors and chocolates for the infants. Even the children in the Children's Hospital were not forgotten. They would receive chocolates too.

The day arrived, and at Cammell Lairds the King and Queen saw men busy on orders for the Admiralty. They had only recently completed several cruisers and destroyers and the dreadnought, HMS *Audacious*. The yard was preparing for war.

On 5 August war was declared. The local reservists had already mobilised and the shipyards had cancelled their annual holiday. Now recruiting centres opened and volunteers rushed to enlist. Not all were accepted. Those below 5 foot 3 were rejected on grounds of height. Alfred Bigland, Birkenhead's MP, pressed for the local committee to be given permission to recruit men of below regulation size. In consequence, two battalions, the 15th and 16th Cheshire Regiment, were formed of men drawn from all over the country. Known as 'Bigland's Birkenhead Bantams', they wore a circular lapel-badge with the letters 'B.B.B.' together with a cockerel.

The reality of war soon hit the Borough as the wounded began to return. Buildings were requisitioned as temporary hospitals and convalescent homes, among them Manor Hill, Hemingford Street School and the newly completed school in Bidston Avenue. Almost every family had someone in the

125 *A postcard produced to commemorate the royal visit, 25 March 1914. The entrance to Cammell Laird's has been specially decorated.*

BIGLAND'S BIRKENHEAD BANTAMS.

'Where are you going to, my little man?'

'I'm going to France to fight if I can!'

'But you are too small to fight Germans,' I said,

'Just take off your coat and I'll fight you instead.'

'But what is your regiment, may I inquire?'

'The 1st Bigland's Bantams - a name to inspire,

Those men who are longing to prove to the foe,

That their spirits are right if their stature is low.'

Anon, November 1914

126 *Bigland's Bantams.*

127   *King George V and Queen Mary visit Cammell Laird's.*

forces; two complete companies of the RNVR had gone from Cammell Lairds alone. The men who remained behind worked long hours repairing damaged ships and turning out new ones. By 1916 four E-class submarines had been launched and by 1918 two L-class and an R12. So crucial was the contribution of the yard to the war effort that the King and Queen made a second visit on 14 March 1917. Cammell Lairds' output of war shipping up to that spring was in excess of 150,000 tons.

All shipping was at risk. The *Lusitania*, a Cunard liner with local people among her crew, was torpedoed by a German submarine on 7 May 1915. As news of her sinking spread there was an outbreak of anti-German rioting. Shops owned by German families were attacked, their windows smashed and their stock looted. Among the victims were Otto Krook,

a pork butcher in Camden Street, and Emile Strauss, an Oxton hairdresser. Even in the suburbs members of the Gostenhofer family were mobbed for their German-sounding name.

WAR WORK

The Borough's women played an important part in the war effort. The WSS abandoned its campaign for votes and its members involved themselves in relief work, nursing and gardening, or entered jobs which had previously been the preserve of men. To cater for this new workforce a Day Nursery was opened in Cole Street. Babies as young as one month old could be left there from 7.30 a.m. to 7 p.m., the long day reflecting the hours their mothers worked.

With so many of their male employees away fighting, the public services turned to women. In May 1915

all, the Borough elected its first woman councillor, Miss Annie Laird.

Voluntary effort was also important. Woollen 'comforts' were knitted—socks, mufflers, helmets and mitts—and felt slippers were stitched. Parcels were packed up and countless letters despatched to the men at the front and POWs. Fundraising was a regular activity and the *Birkenhead News* reported on Flag Days, Bazaars, Concerts, Whist Drives, Garden Fêtes and Sales of Work, all intended to generate money for the troops.

WARTIME SHORTAGES

As the war dragged on, shortages became an increasing problem. There were campaigns to save waste paper and the Allotment Association headed the drive to produce more food. In August 1916 the *Birkenhead News* reported a rise in the cost of a 2lb loaf to 4d. By December 1916 the situation was so serious the Council took steps to use its own parks and open spaces. In January 1917 spare land throughout the Borough came under Cultivation Orders and was divided into allotments. Cricket pitches, football fields and private lawns were dug up to grow fruit and vegetables or else were mown for hay.

Allotments alone were not enough. By March 1917 potatoes were so scarce that the papers reported there were 'practically none procurable'. In April local bakers were banned from wasting flour on fancy cakes and pastries. By November the price of milk had reached 6½d. a quart, and in the YMCA special 'food economy' lectures were organised, but further restrictions were needed. In January 1918 the Corporation was given the power to impose rationing. In February it rationed meat to ¾lb a week, but almost immediately cut this

128 *Stone in Birkenhead Park. The inscription, in Welsh and English, reads: 'This Stone—the gift of Councillor David Evans—Commemorates the Proclamation on this Site of the National Eisteddfod of the Year 1917.'*

female ticket collectors were taken on by the Mersey Railway, and six girl conductors joined the Corporation trams. In the following year women were employed as street cleaners, and in 1917 Birkenhead's Chief Constable enrolled 12 women constables to fill vacancies in his force. At the end of the year, and most ground-breaking of

129 *The Wilfred Owen memorial window,*
installed in the Central Library, 1995, designed by
David Hillhouse.

to ½lb, plus an allowance of 4oz of margarine. Ration cards and coupons were carefully collected.

Fuel, too, was scarce. Everything depended on coal and a local committee was set up to allocate supplies to factories, the ferries, the trams and the generating stations. Services were reduced on both the Mersey Railway and the Borough's trams, and a number of tram stops were cut out. In the home things were desperate. The winter of 1916/17 was one of exceptional cold. Fallen timber was gathered in the parks and people queued to buy tar-covered wooden road blocks from the Corporation Depot in Cleveland Street. When a Coal Rationing Order was imposed in July 1918 people looked forward with dread to another winter.

The Armistice was finally signed in November. In the river ships sounded their sirens, while outside the Town Hall people gathered to rejoice, but their euphoria was short-lived. The reality was sombre. Over the course of the war the Borough's press had recorded some 6,000 servicemen killed, wounded, missing or taken prisoner of war. When the final count came and the cenotaph in Hamilton Square was formally unveiled in 1925 it bore the names of 1,293 killed in the fighting.

In the town's Central Library is another memorial, a vast stained-glass window, bright with the red of poppies, honouring Wilfred Owen, one of Birkenhead's most famous sons. Though not born in the Borough, Owen had lived there for ten years. Central to the

130 *Sculpture*
by H. Tyson
Smith, on the
Birkenhead
Cenotaph,
Hamilton Square.

window is the compelling image of a
soldier blinded by gas, recalling Owen's
description of a gas attack in his poem
'Dulce et Decorum Est'. It includes
Owen's own words, 'My subject is War,
and the pity of War'. Owen was killed
on 4 November 1918, aged 25, just a
week before the war ended.

BETWEEN THE WARS

The transition to peace was not smooth.
With controls ended food prices soared,
and returning servicemen increased the
competition for jobs. Workers became
politicised and even the police force
felt disaffected. On 1 August 1919,
114 members of the Birkenhead force
joined the national police strike. This
was a serious challenge to authority.
Shops were looted and rioting and
damage to property was widespread.
Eventually troops were called in and
special constables used to control the
crowds. Over 300 arrests were made but
not until 18 August was order restored.
All those policemen who had joined the
strike were dismissed from the force.

On a more positive note the Corporation's plan for operating motor buses,
approved in 1914 but delayed by the
war, now began. In July 1919 the first
bus ran between Rock Ferry and Park
Station. Other routes followed, reaching
beyond the Borough to Moreton, Upton,
Port Sunlight and Wallasey in a deliberate
attempt to attract shoppers to the centre
of Birkenhead. Gradually buses replaced
the electric trams, the last of which ran
in July 1937.

Another improvement was the water
supply, a real problem during the war
years when supplies had been rationed
to 4½ hours a day. The scheme to build
the Alwen Dam and bring water from
North Wales had started before the war.
Now it was completed and the supply
was inaugurated on 15 August 1921.

The housing programme was also
resumed. The Gilbrook Estate, first
planned in 1917, was completed and
more housing developed on either side
of the Hoylake Road. The 324 flats
in the Dock Cottages, now 80 years
old, were acquired by the Council and

131 *Private housing
going up on Manor Hill
in the grounds of the
former Manor House.
In the foreground is
Trinity Presbyterian
Church, Alton Road,
now joined with the
former Palm Grove
Methodist Church. The
large buildings adjacent
to the church are those
of Birkenhead High
School.*

refurbished, and in Tranmere 400 houses were built for sale. Private housing, too, spread through the suburbs. Fields disappeared and large old mansions, like Lingdale and Jackson's Manor House, were demolished and their grounds developed with semi–detached properties. At the Priory the renovations begun in 1913 were completed and the refurbished Chapter House was dedicated as a chapel in July 1919.

National legislation drove other changes. The 1918 Education Act raised the school leaving age to 14, and to accommodate the older pupils six new Central Schools were built or adapted. The Borough's annual education budget doubled in three years, rising from £79,589 in 1919 to £159,236 in 1922.

LEISURE, RECREATION AND SPORT

The post-war years saw the rise of cinema and radio. In 1919 the old Theatre Royal closed and reopened as the Scala, to be followed by a series of purpose-built cinemas. At their peak of popularity there were 14 in the town. From the Argyle came the first live broadcast of a radio show in 1931.

Football, too, attracted a growing number of followers. Though fixtures had been difficult, Tranmere Rovers had survived the war as so many of its players were in reserved occupations. Before 1914 it had only competed in local leagues but in 1919 it succeeded Leeds City in the Central League and by 1921 had joined the northern section of the newly formed Football League's Division 3.

In the '20s the Borough gained a new Art Gallery and Museum in Slatey Road, funded by the Williamson Bequest. John Williamson had been a

132   *The Argyle Theatre played a pioneering role in live radio broadcasting.*

director of Cunard and, together with his son Patrick, had left the Borough a legacy of £40,000. The collections were transferred from the old art gallery in Hamilton Street and the new building opened to the public on 1 December 1928.

In the summer of the following year the Scouts organised a World Jamboree for their 'Coming of Age' in the grounds of Arrowe Park, its 450 acres provided free by the Corporation. Over 56,000 scouts attended the camp, coming from all over the world. They were visited by the Prince of Wales, later Edward VIII, and their newspaper, the *Daily Arrow*, sold 38,000 copies. Despite the almost continuous rain and the need to evacuate

133 *The 1921-2 team photo. Tranmere Rovers had just joined the Football League and were about to kick off for their very first game at Prenton Park, against Crewe Alexandra, whom they beat 4:1.*

134 *The Williamson Art Gallery.*

135 *Scouts at the Jamboree.*

some of the boys, the two weeks of the camp were recalled with great nostalgia by those who were there.

RECESSION

The Jamboree took place just in time. In October 1929 came the Wall Street Crash, which brought hard times for everyone. Cammell Laird, like other shipbuilders, was in crisis as orders were cancelled, and activity in the Docks dwindled to almost nothing as trade declined. Workers were put on short-time, unemployment doubled and there was a general air of hopelessness throughout the Borough. The congregation of Trinity Presbyterian Church in Alton Road opened a 'Fund for Poor Families'. Other charities offered help but no one could provide work. In January 1932 the *Birkenhead News* reported the tragic case of an unemployed mechanic found hanging from a tree in Tranmere Woods. He had been without a job for 15 months.

In 1929 the old Board of Guardians had been wound up and its functions transferred to the Council, which was now responsible for administering relief through its Public Assistance Committee. Despite the problems of the Borough there was antipathy among ratepayers towards 'dole scroungers' and some of them still supported the means test. Thus, weekly payments of relief in Birkenhead were some 3s. below those paid in other areas.

By the autumn of 1932 there were serious disturbances in the Borough. Some 5,000 unemployed workers marched on the Public Assistance Offices in Conway Street, demanding an increase in payments. Getting no satisfaction the demonstrators moved on to the house of Alderman Baker, Chairman of the PAC, where they clashed with the police, and a number of men were arrested. More

demonstrations followed, lasting a further three days. Then, in an attempt to ease the crisis, the Public Assistance Committee agreed to raise weekly payments from 12s. to 15s. 3d. for men, and from 10s. to 13s. 6d. for women. At the same time both the Council and the Mersey Docks & Harbour Company put in hand various public work schemes aimed at providing employment.

One scheme was already in progress. A Mersey Road Tunnel had first been proposed in 1922, with the aim of improving communications between Liverpool and Birkenhead. In 1925 the work was approved and Parliament voted £2½ million towards the cost from central government funds. It also granted permission to charge tolls for 20 years. The toll was never relaxed and is still charged today.

Work had started on the tunnel just before Christmas 1925, with digging taking place on both sides. Twenty-seven months later the tunnellers met, and on 3 April 1928 the mayors of Liverpool and Birkenhead, wearing their chains of office but protected from the dripping rock by stout oilskins and sou'westers, were able to shake hands, having come from their respective sides of the river.

Fortunately for the unemployed there was still much to do and work continued on the tunnel until 1934. The official opening was on 18 July. Crowds stood and cheered King George V and Queen Mary as they made their way through the tunnel from Liverpool and proceeded on to open the new Central Library in Borough Road. The old Carnegie Library had been a casualty of the tunnel scheme, demolished to make way for the tunnel approach, but £55,000 was paid in compensation and the present Library erected in its place. Another casualty was

136   *Aerial view of central Birkenhead, showing the new tunnel approach. Preparations are being made for the official opening on 18 July 1934.*

the 'luggage boat service'. With a tunnel only tankers and horse-drawn vehicles used the ferry.

A further public works scheme designed to ease unemployment was the creation of the Bidston Dock and the replacement of the existing swing bridges with bascule bridges. The dock, the last in the Birkenhead system, opened in 1933 but has now been filled in, despite a petition by environmentalists to retain it as an area of open wetland.

The '30s marked a turning point in the history of the Borough. The census of 1931 recorded a peak in population of 147,946. In subsequent years numbers declined as people moved out to the suburbs or went further afield in search of work.

137 *The new Central Library, Borough Road.*

In 1935 came the Silver Jubilee celebrations. In the following year George V died and the town heard first the proclamation of Edward VIII as king and then his abdication speech. In 1936 celebrations for the coronation of his brother, George VI, were held.

CAMMELL LAIRDS
Employment picked up in the later 1930s as the navy began to re-arm. In 1935 Cammell Laird won the order for HMS *Ark Royal*, the first purpose-built aircraft carrier. Costing nearly £3 million to construct, it was launched in April 1937, watched by some 30,000 people. As the great ship slid into the Mersey it must have been clear that the outbreak of war was just a matter of time.

138 *(Left) The road tunnel in use.*

139 *(Right) The road tunnel's ancillary buildings, including the Woodside, Sidney Street and Taylor Street ventilation shafts, were designed by the eminent Liverpool architect, Herbert J. Rowse.*

140   *The* Ark Royal *in the Gladstone Dock.*

The *Ark Royal* assisted in the sinking of the *Bismarck* but was eventually torpedoed in the Mediterranean in 1941. Another tragic loss took place much closer to home and before war actually broke out, the sinking of the submarine HMS *Thetis* in the summer of 1939. *Thetis* was a T-class submarine built at Cammell Laird. While undertaking sea trials in Liverpool Bay she was accidentally flooded and the inrush of water caused her bow to sink to the seabed. Although the stern remained visible at the surface, only four of her crew escaped. The remaining 99 lost their lives in what was the worst submarine tragedy in British waters. A memorial to those who drowned can be found in the tower of St Mary's Church. Alongside the spiral staircase are all their names, officers and ratings, servicemen and civilians, in strict alphabetical order with no one man given precedence over another.

141   *The tragedy of the submarine* Thetis *presaged the huge loss of life experienced during the war itself.*

AIR RAID PROTECTION
AND EVACUATION

For the authorities the great fear was attack from the air. In Birkenhead an Air Raid Precautions Committee was formed and in September 1938 it issued an information leaflet. People were told how to deal with incendiary bombs, high explosive bombs and gas and urged to blackout their homes, fill sand and water buckets to put out fires and, if they lacked a suitable 'place of refuge', even dig trenches on their premises. Appeals were made for Air Raid Wardens and Auxiliary Firemen and for volunteers to join Rescue Parties and First Aid Teams. Reassurance was given that the Council would provide Public Shelters in the parks and a warning was given that sections of the population might have to be evacuated.

Plans for evacuation were already in hand. The whole of Birkenhead bounded by the river, the Docks and the east side of the Bidston ridge was designated an 'Evacuable Area'. All schoolchildren from within this zone were to be moved to safe areas in Shropshire and in northern and central Wales. One of the scheduled

'safe areas' was Connah's Quay, in Flintshire, the home of RAF Sealand and the John Summers' Steelworks. The Education Committee justifiably felt that these 'targets' were as much at risk as Birkenhead and had Connah's Quay removed from the list.

Responsibility for all the arrangements fell on the Borough's Evacuation Officer, Mr E.W. Tame, the Town Clerk, and Mr G.B. Dempsey, the Director of Education. Knowing that needy families might have difficulty in providing their children with clothing, schools were advised to collect spare garments and devote needlework lessons to making 'warm clothing, small bags, towels, etc'. Appeals for clothes were also made through the *Birkenhead News and Advertiser.* Ever practical, the Education Office issued orders regarding 'school pets'. Under no circumstances were these to accompany the children to the safe areas. Arrangements must be made in advance for 'their disposal', however upsetting this might be.

Before the summer holidays schools had issued families with a kit list and suggestions for food to be taken on the journey:

142 *Evacuee children were carefully labelled.*

To be brought by each Child

Change of under clothing; night clothes; house shoes or slippers or plimsolls; a change of socks or stockings; toothbrush, hairbrush; comb; towel; soap; handkerchiefs; stamped addressed postcard and the ANTI GAS RESPIRATOR complete with box in a suitable form of carrier which can be slung over the shoulder.
Sandwiches—egg or cheese
Packets of nuts and seedless raisins

In late August the schools reopened and some, including Brassey Street, Conway Street and Ionic Street, even practised walking their children in a crocodile to their entraining station. Then, on the last day of the month, came the final orders:

URGENT
BIRKENHEAD EDUCATION COMMITTEE

Final Evacuation Order received to-day 31st August 12-15 p.m.

Evacuation therefore begins to-morrow Friday, the 1st September which is the first day according to the time-table. Saturday is the second day, Sunday the third day and Monday the fourth day.

Headteachers will take all necessary steps and instruct all evacuable scholars, teachers, helpers and mothers with young children concerned as to the place and time of assembly, etc.

Kit, respirators and food for day to be taken.

Teachers not accompanying their school to the Reception. Areas will assist in entraining and will report at the Education Offices for instruction at 9 a.m. daily thereafter.

Director of Education

In fact the evacuation process lasted five days, with 11,709 children and 3,049 teachers, mothers and helpers leaving the town for their billets in the country. On 6 September the headlines in the *Birkenhead News* proclaimed, 'Town without children, evacuation complete.'

SECOND WORLD WAR

For the first few months no bombs fell and some of the evacuees returned home. In the town various manufacturers switched to war work. At Lee's Tapestry Works the Jacquard looms turned over to weaving khaki and canvas and the braid looms made webbing. Alcock's, the sticking plaster firm, moved into the embroidery room, manufacturing parachutes and barrage balloons.

The first raids came the following summer. As the Battle of Britain raged in the south, bombs began falling on Birkenhead. On the night of 9 August 1940 a young woman was killed in Prenton, the first fatality on Merseyside. On 12 August bombs fell on the Docks and for the next few months raids were common. Though many people had their own Morrison or Anderson shelters, others took refuge in Public Shelters or went underground. Unofficial shelters included Hamilton Square Station, the Market vaults and the cellars of the Birkenhead Brewery in Oxton Road. In Bidston and Tranmere deep public shelters had been blasted out of the solid rock and their network of passages could accommodate several thousand people.

Twice in 1940 the town was visited by King George and Queen Elizabeth. In August they went to Cammell Laird and in November they toured bombed areas in the town. Among the public buildings destroyed in the raids was the famous

143 *'Any Old Iron?' Iron railings disappeared from the Borough during the war years.*

Any Old Iron?

There is a vital and urgent need for scrap iron of all descriptions for the manufacture of tanks and householders in Birkenhead and Wirral are asked by the authorities to turn out any scrap metal they may have in their possession and notify their local authority, who will make arrangements for its collection. The dustmen employed by the Corporation Cleansing Department have been instructed to take away any scrap iron collected by householders, and similar arrangements are being made by other authorities in Wirral.

Argyle Theatre, where stars like Harry Lauder and George Formby had once performed. On the night in question, 1 September 1940, the key attraction was 'Billy Scott Coomber with his singing Grenadiers'. Their performance finished with the singing of 'There'll Always be an England', but this would be the last song ever sung at the Argyle. By the end of the night the theatre was a burned-out ruin.

Worse was to come. On 12/13 March 1941, 40 land mines and 180 heavy bombs fell. Over the month as a whole 228 people were killed and 275 seriously injured. Again, in the first week of May, the so-called 'May Blitz' caused widespread destruction. Woodchurch Road School was badly damaged and a direct hit on the school shelter killed eight people. For the townspeople left with damaged homes and no gas, water or electricity, the WVS, based in Atherton Street, ran rest centres and toured the town with their mobile canteens. In addition, the Communal Feeding Committee ran several British Restaurants. The last bombs fell on Birkenhead in November 1941 but it would be years before all the damage was repaired. In total over 450 individuals had been killed, some 26,000 buildings affected and 2,079 dwellings destroyed.

144 *Bomb damage to St Saviour's Church, Oxton. The original Caernarvon Castle pub was destroyed in the same raid.*

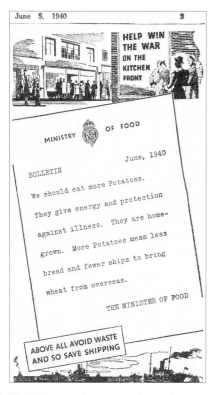

145   *Winning the war on the Kitchen Front.*

Though the raids were over, the war dragged on. Rationing was the concern of the Council's Food Control Committee. By the end of 1941, butter, bacon, sugar, meat, tea, margarine, cooking fat, cheese, jam, marmalade, treacle, syrup and clothing all required coupons. As in the First World War, great emphasis was placed on 'Digging for Victory' and open areas were taken over for allotments. In 1942 the arrival of contingents of Americans, billeted in the transit camp in Arrowe Park, brought excitement and offers of chocolate, chewing gum and nylons. For most people at the time these were unheard of luxuries.

VICTORY

The end of the war was celebrated throughout the Borough. Blackout restrictions were lifted and street parties arranged: 'Iced cakes, ice cream, jellies and lemonade appeared as if by magic, to be followed by music, dancing, fireworks and illuminations. Neighbours worked hard to achieve these great results, pooling meagre rations and lending precious crockery and furniture.' On 8 May, VE night, the Town Hall and Hamilton Square were festooned with lights. Hundreds of people gathered in the square to celebrate. On VJ night the decorations were even more elaborate and crowds came from all over Merseyside. An enormous Union Jack was draped from the Town Hall balcony and over 6,000 lights were strung round the Square. Prime among the attractions was the huge 'V' formed by searchlights, their beams almost blinding in red, white and blue. No one could remember a night like it.

146   *VE Night in Hamilton Square.*

11

Challenge and Change

People had looked forward to the end of the war but peacetime brought its own austerity. Rationing continued and food shortages increased. Bread and flour, which had never been rationed in the war years, were now restricted and the philosophy of 'Make do and Mend' seemed bound to continue.

POST-WAR PROBLEMS—HOUSING

For the Corporation the most acute problem was the shortage of houses. Bomb damage had affected over 28,000 homes, the slum clearance programmes begun before the war had been suspended and the backlog of repairs was enormous. At the same time bricks were almost unobtainable, most brickyards having closed during the war because of the impossibility of blacking out the glare from their kilns. Bricklayers, too, were in short supply. The process of demobilisation was a long one and many tradesmen were still in the forces.

As a short-term solution the Estates Committee decided to build 'temporary bungalows'. By 1946, 342 of the appropriately named 'Phoenix' prefabs had been erected, the first going up on a blitzed site between Price Street and Beckwith Street, near Park Station.

By the following year more had been built, giving a total of 506. Originally intended to last ten years, they were so well designed (they even included an Electrolux fridge) that many continued in use until the 1960s.

Work also resumed in the North End, where the century-old Dock Cottages demolished before the war were in the process of being replaced by houses and flats. The flats were low-rise walk-up blocks, three or four storeys high, and included what would become the notorious Ilchester Square.

Still more homes were needed and the Council turned its attention to the edge of its built-up area. In 1928 its boundaries had been extended to embrace the civil parishes of Landican, Thingwall, Prenton and Ford. In 1933 Noctorum, Woodchurch and parts of Arrowe, Bidston and Upton were also added. By the war the Borough was double its original size, with plenty of room into which to expand. In 1939 new housing was planned for the Mount Estate, where building now began. Plans were also drawn up for Woodchurch, Prenton Dell, Overchurch and Thingwall.

It was the scheme for Woodchurch that attracted national attention. In 1926 an

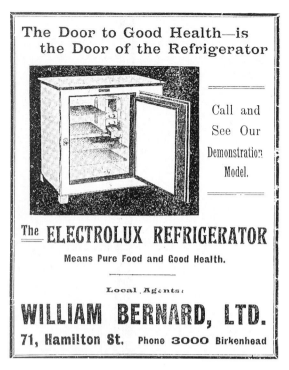
147   *Electrolux Refrigerators were provided
in the prefabs.*

area of farmland and a cluster of cottages grouped round Holy Cross Church had been sold to Birkenhead by Sir Ernest Royden. One plot had been bought by the Co-op for a laundry, but lack of funds and inadequate drainage meant the rest had remained undeveloped. Then, just before war ended, the Council instructed Bertie Robinson, its Borough Engineer,

148   *The last remnant of the walk-up flats at Ilchester
Square, built to replace the Dock Cottages.*

to prepare plans for a housing estate. At the same time it approached Professor (later Sir) Charles H. Reilly, formerly head of the School of Architecture at Liverpool University, to produce a planning scheme for the Borough as a whole.

It was while preparing this scheme that Reilly claims to have seen plans for the Woodchurch estate, presumably those drawn up by Robinson and already approved by the Council. Ignoring this, Reilly immediately produced a layout of his own. Whereas Robinson's plan was for an estate laid out along traditional Garden City lines, Reilly's alternative was much more revolutionary, consisting of dwellings grouped round a series of communal 'village greens'. The Council was now faced with adjudicating between the two and opinions were divided. The Conservatives were anxious to press ahead with the scheme already approved, while Labour members, led by Alderman C. McVey, favoured Reilly. Thus began the 'Battle of the Plans', a debate that reached the national press. 'The whole of England should watch Birkenhead's decision,' said an editorial in the *London Evening Standard*.

After much heated debate the Council finally adopted Robinson's plan, but had still to find an architect for the houses. On the recommendation of RIBA they appointed Herbert J. Rowse, already known in the Borough for his Art Deco tunnel entrances and the brick-faced ventilation stations. Rowse confounded everyone by producing yet another layout and it was this third scheme, planned on Garden City lines, that was finally approved. Work began in 1946 and the first houses were ready for occupation in 1947. By 1953 the 1,000th house, 'Coronation Villa', had

149 *The demo-lition of Oak and Eldon Gardens, 30 September 1979.*

been completed and the key handed over by Percy Collick, MP.

Even peripheral estates could not solve the whole housing crisis and, like other authorities, Birkenhead began to build upwards. Multi-storey flats seemed the solution to the pressing problems of run-down terraced housing lacking bathrooms or inside toilets and badly in need of refurbishment. No one looked to 'renovation' as an alternative, and whole communities were swept away. The first targets were Oak Street and Eldon Place.

Plans to clear the area had been prepared before the war. 'Oak Street will soon disappear as the houses are to be demolished,' reported the St Laurence's Notice Book in 1936, adding, 'this is not just slum clearance; it was the violent rupture of a close network of deep relationships between friends and relatives'.

Such wisdom was ignored. Soon the infamous Oak and Eldon Gardens, built

on stilts and rising ten storeys high, began to tower over the neighbourhood. In April 1958 came their official opening, presided over again by Percy Collick. Only twenty years later the flats were demolished, victims of crime, vandalism and poor maintenance. But all that was in the future. It was with a sense of optimism that the first tenant accepted his key and soon other tower blocks followed.

EDUCATION

In 1944 the Butler Education Act reshaped the structure of education. It raised the school leaving age to 15 and replaced the old system of 'elementary' and 'higher' education with one of primary, secondary and further education. For Birkenhead's children there was now the dreaded 'Eleven-plus', an examination devised as a means of selecting children for the school thought best geared to their abilities. To conform to the Act,

150 *Mural by Eric Kennington illustrating Birkenhead's history, from the former Birkenhead Technical College, Borough Road.*

the Council's six Central schools were redesignated 'Secondary Moderns', as were St Hugh's RC School and Our Lady in Tollemache Road. At the same time Birkenhead Institute, Rock Ferry, Park High School for Boys and the Girls Secondary School in Park Road South were all confirmed as grammar schools. Free places were also available through a system of direct grants at Birkenhead School, St Anselm's, Holt Hill Convent and Birkenhead High School.

The Holt Technical College, which for over fifty years had occupied the former Tranmere District Offices in Leighton Road, was to be replaced. Work began on a new college in Borough Road in 1949 and in 1950 Queen Elizabeth, the Queen Consort, laid a commemorative stone. In 1955 Sir Harry (later Lord) Cohen, a former pupil of Birkenhead Institute and Professor of Medicine at Liverpool University, performed the official opening. For the next half century the 'Tech' was the focus of further education in the town and, for a time at least, its hall served as the Glenda Jackson Theatre. Unknown to many, its basement was designed as a bunker ready to be used in the event of a nuclear war.

THE DOCKS AND THE SHIPYARDS

The '50s and early '60s were boom years. In the immediate post-war period both the Docks and the shipyards were busy. The Docks had suffered a battering during the war but now benefited from the export drive and the resurgence of trade with Africa and the Far East. The Vittoria Dock was enlarged to provide improved berthing facilities and Bidston Dock was adapted to handle iron ore. At the same time the Lairages, a major importing point for cattle, continued to handle up to 2,000 head a day.

At Cammell Lairds there was no shortage of work as damaged stock was repaired and passenger ships, commandeered as troop carriers, were refitted for civilian use. At the same time came orders for tankers, ore-carriers and ferries, and more work from the navy, including the 10-year task of replacing the aircraft carrier *Ark Royal*.

One unusual commission was the fitting out of HMS *Campania* for the Sea

Travelling Exhibition of the Festival of Britain. Originally a refrigerated cargo ship, *Campania* had been converted to an aircraft carrier during the war. In 1951 she carried a floating exhibition to ten coastal cities and towns, including Birkenhead. Thousands of people visited her in Bidston Dock as well as attending a programme of special events including a 'Festival Variety Show' and a 'Festival Serenade'.

In 1953 Cammell Laird and Company (Shipbuilding & Engineering) Ltd registered as a company in its own right, leaving Cammell Laird & Co. Ltd as its holding company. It then embarked on an ambitious programme of reconstruction, designed to cater for the new supertankers. The yard was extended onto reclaimed land to the south and a huge dry dock was excavated from the sandstone to the north. Parts of Church Street were removed as was a section of St Mary's graveyard, the bodies buried there being reinterred at Landican Cemetery. In 1962 the dock was completed and officially opened by Princess Alexandra.

Another venture was the standardisation of design. To save costs, clients could choose one of six 'off the peg' ships: three dry cargo carriers, two bulk carriers and a tanker. At the same time the yard merged with its neighbours, Grayson, Rollo and Clover Docks Ltd, Ship Repairers. Subsequently, Grayson's was renamed Cammell Laird (Shiprepairers) Ltd, and it took over most of the company's repair work.

Despite these improvements Cammell Lairds, like other British shipbuilders, was finding it difficult to maintain its place in the world market. It had also suffered a serious demarcation dispute and labour relations were poor, but for a time the order book was cushioned by government help. In the '60s the firm received orders for two Polaris submarines, HMS *Renown* and HMS *Revenge*,

151 *The old St Mary's graveyard was almost totally removed to make way for the new dock, opened in 1962.*

and the submarine HMS *Conqueror*, and by 1969 was employing 11,400 men. But without government subsidies this level of activity could not last.

ROAD TRANSPORT AND RETAILING

Petrol rationing had continued after the war, curbing any expansion there might have been in private motoring. At the same time nationalisation had given British Rail a temporary monopoly on the carriage of goods. When this ceased, the impact on the road tunnel was immediate. The last luggage boat had run from Woodside in 1941 and the last sailed from Wallasey in 1947. From then on all cross-river road traffic converged

on Birkenhead and congestion at the tunnel approach was enormous. The existing roads were unable to cope, especially during rush hour.

In 1964 traffic engineers devised a scheme to alleviate this, segregating tunnel traffic from other road users. A complex network of one-way streets and flyovers was approved and formally inaugurated in 1967 by Barbara Castle, Minister of Transport. Inevitably, as had been the case when the tunnel first opened, whole swathes of streets disappeared, interesting buildings were lost and the Edward VII Memorial Clock was relocated.

Other work was also in progress. In 1969 a new Social Services Centre was opened by Lord Cohen and new Municipal Offices by Alderman Oates. By 1969 the tunnel scheme, too, was complete and the official opening was performed by Alderman Hugh Platt, a Freeman of the Borough and the Leader of the Council since 1949. The flyovers he 'opened' were demolished three decades later, condemned, ironically, for the traffic congestion they caused.

Increased car ownership also affected the town centre. Plans were put forward to pedestrianise Grange Road, the main shopping thoroughfare, and to build a shopping precinct and provide car parking space off Claughton Road. The Victorian Market, isolated by the tunnel approach roads, was to be relocated to a new covered hall and its former site made available for office development.

Faced with these changes, some of the older family businesses survived but others were eased out by major retailers. Shops built in the town's most prosperous period were demolished, as was St John's Church, dating from the 1840s and now only remembered in

152 *Demolition in central Birkenhead. Whole swathes of terrace housing were swept away as part of various regeneration programmes.*

the name 'St John's Square'. Subsequent years saw further developments. A large superstore, a multi-storey car-park and the ambitiously named Pyramids shopping centre all appeared.

REORGANISATION OF LOCAL GOVERNMENT—THE LOSS OF IDENTITY

In 1973 Alderman Roberts, Leader of both the Labour Group and the Town Council, officially opened Birkenhead's new Fire Service and Ambulance Headquarters in Exmouth Street. This would be one of the last civic ceremonies organised by the Council, for on 1 April 1974, a date some thought significant, the County Borough of Birkenhead ceased to exist.

Since the reign of William IV, the town had organised its own affairs, first through the Improvement Commissioners and then through the Corporation. Following reorganisation, its Council merged with those of Wallasey, Bebington, Hoylake and Wirral to form the Metropolitan District of Wirral. This, together with Liverpool, St Helens, Knowsley and Sefton, would now constitute the new County of Merseyside.

Before reorganisation, each of Wirral's districts had provided its own council services. Now these were amalgamated and for reasons of size the new Wirral Council chose Wallasey Town Hall as its base. Wallasey's Council Chamber was bigger and the building itself more modern than that of Birkenhead. For some years the former Town Hall continued as council offices, then in 1991 the computers and filing cabinets moved out and the once proud building, over a century old, lost its administrative function.

DECLINE

The new authority inherited numerous problems. Even before it took over it was clear that much of Birkenhead's new housing was failing to fulfil its initial promise. Within a year of reorganisation the tenants of Oak and Eldon Gardens had to be rehoused. On the peripheral estates things were little better. At Woodchurch, planned with such optimism, Rouse's award-winning designs had been abandoned for cheaper housing and high-rise flats, and the local press was describing the estate as 'trouble torn' and a 'forgotten city'.

At Noctorum buildings that had been up scarcely ten years revealed fundamental structural weaknesses as slabs of concrete fell from their walls. Repairs were out of the question and Wirral Council was forced to demolish 17 blocks of the so-called 'rat box flats'.

The situation on the Ford Estate, planned for 6,000 people, was even more acute. In 1969 the *Birkenhead News* reported on its lack of facilities:

> The estate consists of houses and flats, roads and pavements, street lamps and trees—and that is all … There are no telephones, no post boxes, no shops, no pubs and few buses. Mobile shops do visit the area but for the thousand and one things the vans cannot supply, the housewife has to go a long way to do her shopping.

By the '80s the condition of the estate was making the national press. To remedy this, houses were replanned and a new name, 'Beechwood', chosen to give 'the Ford' a better image.

Even the Municipal Offices were not immune from the legacy of poor building methods. The multi-storey block on the corner of Cleveland Street had been faced with panels of orange mosaic and nicknamed 'Golden Towers'. When window frames and panels began falling to the ground the tower was demolished and only the lower storey retained.

A more fundamental problem was rising unemployment. The railway, once a major employer, had lost most of its freight traffic to the roads, and miles of rusting sidings now lay idle. Woodside Station closed in 1967 and, with the exception of the Bidston-Shotton line, the local rail network assumed a 'passengers only' character. Other employment also vanished. The Birkenhead Brewery, taken over by Threlfalls', brewed its last beer in 1968. Lees, so long the mainstay of the North End, closed in 1970, unable to find markets for its fine textiles, and the site of its weaving sheds becoming a cut-price supermarket.

Employment on the Docks also declined. Patterns of trade were shifting and new technology brought a reduced demand for traditional labour. Passenger liners vanished as air transport took their trade. Cargo handling became increasingly mechanised and ships themselves were larger and fewer as their turnaround times improved. The real blow came in 1972 when the Mersey Docks and Harbour Board, now reconstituted as the Mersey Docks and Harbour Company, opened a purpose-built container port, the Royal Seaforth, on the opposite side of the river. With the increasing use of containers and the opening of the Seaforth grain terminal, premises on the East and West Float closed and large sections of Birkenhead's dockland became redundant and derelict.

Most fundamental of all were the changes at Cammell Lairds. In 1970 the government took a 50 per cent share in the yard and two years later backed a further programme of modernisation, including the building of a huge covered construction hall. In 1977 the firm was nationalised, becoming part of British Shipbuilders, and in the following year received orders for three destroyers. The reprieve was short-lived. By 1980 the *Birkenhead News* described the yard as 'desperately short of merchant orders and with only one type 42 destroyer on the stocks'. The jobless total for the town was twice the national average.

A change of direction seemed to offer hope and in 1981 work began on the oil rig, *Sovereign Explorer*, its huge structure visible from all over the town. But the blow fell again. In 1985 the yard was denationalised, becoming a mere subsidiary of Vickers Shipbuilding and Engineering (VSEL). From then on orders dwindled, and from a peak of 16,000 workers at the end of the Second World War, the workforce dropped to under 2,000 by 1990. In 1993, when a tug towed HMS *Unicorn* out to the river, onlookers read the message on its stern: 'The End'. On 30 July 1993 the yard ceased trading, and though new owners reopened the yard they, too, were unsuccessful. It changed hands again, finally being bought by Peel Holdings early in 2007.

REGENERATION

Through all this the Council worked hard to attract jobs to the area and to seek outside funding to remedy the acute social and physical dereliction of parts of the town. In 1979 it gained a good ally in the principled and independently minded Frank Field, elected MP on the retirement of Edmund Dell.

153 *Window commemorating the training ship* Conway *in the Conway chapel, Birkenhead Priory.* Conway *was moored off Rock Ferry from 1859 to 1941. Among those it prepared for the sea was the Poet Laureate, John Masefield. The ship was moved to the Menai Straits in the Second World War but broke up after going aground on her way back to the Mersey for a refit in 1953. Training continued on shore until 1974.*

154 *The oil rig,* Sovereign Explorer, *dominates the yard.*

155   *The Grand Entrance looking from Conway Street.*

156   *Italian Lodge, for many years the home of Edward Kemp, Park Superintendent. When their financial problems forced the Commissioners to withdraw his salary Kemp was allowed to remain living in the Lodge.*

157   *The Swiss Bridge.*

158   *View from restored Roman boathouse across the lower lake.*

159   *The restored Roman boathouse.*

160 *The former Birkenhead Town Hall now houses the Wirral Museum.*

In 1981 the Merseyside Development Corporation brought help to Birkenhead's dockland, and from the '90s a bewildering battery of initiatives funnelled regeneration funding into the town. The first of these, 'City Lands', Wirral's City Challenge scheme, ran from 1992 to 1997 and set out to revitalise central Birkenhead. New bus and railway stations were planned as well as a swimming pool, a cinema and modern office blocks. In 1996 the Queen opened the Europa Pools, in 1997 a seven-screen cinema complex appeared and, in an imaginative gesture, the appropriately named Europa Boulevard was lined with trees.

The railway station, the first to be opened for a century, was built between Hamilton Square and Birkenhead Park, providing access to the Market and shopping precinct. Remarkably, the line remained open for most of the construction period, and in 1998 Neil Kinnock, as a European Commissioner, opened the new station, Conway Park.

161 *The Roll-on Roll-off ferry terminal at Twelve Quays is one of the latest additions to the Birkenhead waterfront.*

162   *Looking inland at Woodside Ferry, 2008.*

Of all the regeneration programmes, the most appealing to the historian was focussed on Hamilton Square. The significance of the Square had been recognised in July 1977 when it became one of the first Conservation Areas designated by the new Council. The Square itself was the largest Grade 1 listed Victorian square outside London, and adjacent buildings in Hamilton Street, Argyle Street and Market Streets were also included. An important element in its conservation policy was the clause relating to the wider setting. Fully aware of the threat that the future might hold, the policy required

> all new development located outside but visible from the central square to be of a scale and design appropriate to maintaining its historic character.

The 'Hamilton Quarter' programme ran from 1995 to 2002. Smoke-blackened façades were cleaned, derelict buildings restored and residential accommodation provided in the empty upper storeys of shops in conjunction with a number of housing associations. A Heritage Tramway was laid down, running from the ferry, and work began on a tram depot in Taylor Street. A new centre was opened at Pacific Road, and a programme of concerts and music festivals inaugurated. The former Birkenhead Town Hall, already earmarked for a museum, had its stonework cleaned. Inside, stained-glass windows were repaired, decorative plasterwork repainted, galleries were constructed and displays arranged. On a wet Sunday afternoon in 2001, Wirral Museum was formally opened.

Following the 'Hamilton Quarter', a battery of programmes, all with snappy titles and all operating within fixed time limits, brought further funding to Birkenhead. Training was provided, new technology made available, school-based ITC schemes initiated, living and shopping environments upgraded, and leisure and recreation facilities improved.

FRIENDS AND THE FUTURE

Despite all this some of the most effective work was done by volunteers, friends, groups and societies formed to protect and promote various aspects of Birkenhead's past. Among these are the Birkenhead History Society, founded in 1974, the Friends of Birkenhead Park (1976), the Oxton Society (1979), the friends of Flaybrick Memorial Gardens (1993), the Friends of Bidston Hill (1996) and the Friends of Arrowe Park (2007). Totally independent and with

no self-interest, they act as watchdogs, campaigning to save historic buildings like the Woodside Ferry Terminal or to preserve and enhance open spaces like Bidston Hill or the Park.

As Birkenhead moves further into the 21st century their work is ever more vital. Areas of the waterfront are earmarked as development sites. Peel Holdings, the successor to the Mersey Docks and Harbour Company, have grandiose plans for the docklands and consultants have produced a scheme for Woodside, involving a 'development spine' from the ferry to Hamilton Square.

The old Birkenhead Borough motto was 'Ubi fides ibi lux robur'—'Wherever there is faith there is also light and strength'. At reorganisation Wirral Council adapted it to a new motto, 'By faith and foresight'. Both faith and foresight will be essential if, in planning for the future of Birkenhead, the essence of its past is not swept away.

163   *The Borough of Birkenhead Coat of Arms.*

Select Bibliography

MANUSCRIPT SOURCES

For original material my major sources were the collections in Wirral Archives, including the records of the following:

Birkenhead Improvement Commissioners, 1833-1879
Woodside, North Birkenhead and Liverpool Steam Ferry Company, 1835-1858
Birkenhead Poor Law Union, 1861-1930
Oxton Local Board of Health, 1863-1877
Tranmere Local Board of Health, 1860-1877
Birkenhead Corporation, 1877-1889
Birkenhead County Borough, 1889-1974
Cammell Laird & Co.

Among collections consulted elsewhere were the following:

Birmingham City Archives, Boulton and Watt Collection, for correspondence relating to William Laird's boiler works
Dudley Archives and Local History Service for information on the Horton family
Flintshire Record Office for the title deeds and plans of the Price Estate in Birkenhead
Laird family papers in the possession of the late Miss Marianne Laird
RIBA Library, Victoria and Albert Museum, for the drawings and diaries of Thomas Rickman
The Museum of the Isles, Skye, for information on the early work of James Gillespie Graham

2. PUBLISHED MATERIAL

Birkenhead and its surroundings have been well served with histories.
These include:

Allison, J.E., *Sidelights on Tranmere* (1976)
Aspinall, Henry K., *Birkenhead and its Surroundings* (1903)
Boumphrey, Ian and Marilyn, *Birkenhead at War, 1939-1945* (2001)
Boumphrey, Ian and Marilyn, *Yesterday's Birkenhead, 1860-1960* (2007)
Boumphrey, Ian and Marilyn, *Yesterday's Wirral—Birkenhead, Prenton and Oxton* (1981)
Boumphrey, Ian, *Birkenhead, A Pictorial History* (1995)
Brocklebank, R.T., *Birkenhead, An Illustrated History* (2003)
Gamlin, Hilda, *Memories of Birkenhead* (1892)

Kaighin, J.R., *Bygone Birkenhead* (1925)

McIntyre, W.R.S., *Birkenhead Yesterday and Today* (1948)

Mortimer, W.W., *A History of the Hundred of Wirral* (1847)

Neilson, H.B., *Auld-Lang-Syne* (1935)

Sulley, Philip, *History of Ancient and Modern Birkenhead* (1907)

Other works dealing with specific aspects of Birkenhead's history include:

Birkenhead, 1877-1974, County Borough of Birkenhead (1974)

Bombers over Merseyside, Liverpool Daily Post and Echo (1943)

Chadwick, G.F., *The Works of Sir Joseph Paxton, 1808-1865* (1961)

Hillhouse, D., *Della Robbia Pottery, Birkenhead, 1894-1906*, Metropolitan Borough of Wirral (1981)

Hollett, D., *Men of Iron, The Story of Cammell Laird, Shipbuilders, 1828-1991* (1992)

Hollett, D., *Merseyside & the 19th Century Emigrant Trade to Australia*, Metropolitan Borough of Wirral (1988)

Hyde, F.E., *Liverpool and the Mersey, the Development of a Port, 1700-1970* (1971)

Johnson, A. and Moore, K., *The Tapestry Makers—Life and work at Lee's Tapestry Works, Birkenhead* (1987)

Maund, T.B., *The Birkenhead Railway, [LMS 7& GW Joint]* (2000)

Millar, J., *Thomas Brassey, Railway Builder & Canada Works, Birkenhead* (1993)

Reilly, C. and Aslan, N.J., *Outline Plan for the County Borough of Birkenhead* (1947)

Stewart-Brown, R., *Birkenhead Priory and the Mersey Ferry* (1925)

Thornton, C.E., *The People's Garden: A History of Birkenhead Park*, Metropolitan Borough of Wirral (1983)

Warren, K., *Steel, Ships and Men: Cammell Laird, 1824-1993* (1998)

More general works on Cheshire and Merseyside include:

Aitkenhead, N., Barclay, W.J. *et al*, *British Regional Geology: The Pennines and Adjacent Areas* (2002)

Brennand, M. (ed.), *The Archaeology of North West England* (2006)

Crosby, A., *A History of Cheshire* (1996)

Dodgson, J. McNeil, *The Place Names of Cheshire*, IV, E.P.N.S. (1972)

Greenwood, E.F. (ed.), *Ecology and Landscape Development: A History of the Mersey Basin* (1999)

Griffiths, D., Philpott, R.A. and Egan, G., *Meols, the Archaeology of the North Wirral Coast* (2007)

Harris, B.E. and Thacker, A.T. (eds.), *Victoria History of the County of Chester*, I (1987)

Harris, B.E. (ed.), *Victoria History of the County of Chester*, II (1979)

Harris, B.E. (ed.), *Victoria History of the County of Chester*, III (1980)

Higham, N.J., *A Frontier Landscape—The North West in the Middle Ages* (2004)

Higham, N.J., *The Origins of Cheshire* (1991)

Morgan, Philip (ed.), *Domesday Book: Cheshire* (1978)

Pevsner, N. and Hubbard, E., *The buildings of England: Cheshire* (1971)

Phillips, A.D.M. and C.B., *A New Historical Atlas of Cheshire* (2002)

Van Helmond, M., *Votes for Women: The Events on Merseyside 1870-1928*, National Museums and Galleries on Merseyside (1992)

Index